WORSHIP SERVICES

for youth groups

12 complete thematic and seasonal services

WORSHIP SERVICES
for youth groups

12 complete thematic and seasonal services

Jim Marian

 Youth Specialties

Ⅱ ZondervanPublishingHouse

Grand Rapids, Michigan

A Division of HarperCollinsPublishers

Worship Services for Youth Groups: 12 complete thematic and seasonal services
Copyright © 1996 by Youth Specialties, Inc.

Youth Specialties Books, 1224 Greenfield Dr., El Cajon, CA 92021, are published by Zondervan Publishing House, 5300 Patterson S.E., Grand Rapids, MI 49530.

Library of Congress Cataloging-in-Publication Data

Marian, Jim.
    Worship services for youth groups: 12 complete thematic and seasonal services / Jim Marian.
        p.   cm.
    Includes bibliographical references (p.   ).
    ISBN 0-310-20782-7
    1. Worship (Religious education) 2. Church work with youth. I. Title.
BV1522.M294   1996
264'.00835dc20

96-20118
CIP

ISBN: 0-310-20782-7

Unless otherwise indicated, all Scripture quotations are taken from the *Holy Bible: New International Version (North American Edition)*. Copyright © 1973, 1978, 1984 by the International Bible Society. Used by permission of Zondervan Publishing House.

Edited by Sheri Stanley
Cover and interior design by Rogers Design & Associates

Printed in the United States of America

98 99 00 01 02 03/ /10 9 8 7 6 5

To Lynne, my partner in life and ministry, whose invaluable assistance and creativity made this book possible.

You may contact the author about speaking, leading worship, or conducting a worship leaders workshop in your area by calling his office: 818/795-7221.

Contents

Readings, scripts, and reproducible sheets in this book

Acknowledgements

Thanks to—
- My children, Ross and Brenna, who patiently (well, kind of) allowed their parents to write this book.
- The staff and students of Lake Avenue Church, for the opportunity to worship with them in creative and meaningful ways.
- My coworkers in the high school ministry at Lake Avenue who helped implement the services in this book: Harriet Bogris, Rob Bell, Jim Toole, and Robert Blackman.
- Jeff Wilson, for the Stress Test in service eleven.
- Noel Bechetti, for his patience and support in seeing this book become a reality— and special appreciation to Tim McLaughlin and his team for editing the manuscript.
- My Lord and Savior Jesus Christ, who invites us to worship him in creative and wonderful ways.

What Worship Services for Youth Groups is all about, and how to use it

Like you, I know the feeling of leaving a youth meeting convinced that nothing spiritual happened. Maybe the students enjoyed themselves, but did they meet God in any meaningful way?

As a worship leader for more than a decade, I've seen the impact that authentic worship can have on young people. They may grow up hearing about God and learning about God, but it's finally through worship that they *feel* the reality of God.

My students aren't the only ones. Despite my experience, I'm still apt to pigeonhole worship as merely singing—when, in fact, the Bible is full of creative and wonderful expressions of worship that have nothing to do with singing. Too, the many varieties of Christian faith traditions are rich with worship practices from which we can all learn. *Worship Services for Youth Groups* includes many of these.

The dozen creative worship services in this book are tools for bringing your students into the presence of God. Within the format of these services, you can nudge your students out of their worshipping comfort zone and into interaction with, primarily, God. (Not that worship isn't essentially a community act; it's just that students are no less inclined than adults to forget the Invisible One they came to worship, when there's so much that's visible happening around them.)

So how do you create a worship experience for teenagers?

Imagine your students worshipping like they meant it. What would it look like? What would it feel like? Who would lead it? What elements would be emphasized to help your students focus on God and respond to him in a meaningful and life-changing way?

I've asked myself these same questions in my efforts to facilitate creative worship for my students. And what I've found that distinguishes youth *worship* from a typical youth *meeting* is this: vertical focus.

Youth meetings generally abound in horizontal aspects—games, crowd breakers, Bible studies, small-group discussions—these bring students together for a chance to get to know one another, to learn together, to build a sense of community.

A worship service, on the other hand, has a vertical focus that directs students' attention from each other and to God, if only for a moment. In a worship experience, I believe, students are not spectators but participants, especially as that worship prompts them to respond personally and intimately to God.

What vertical focus *doesn't* mean is that the service is all quiet, all somber, all boring. To the contrary, my students have enjoyed the creativity of these services as they've met the living God.

In fact, students I know—both churched and unchurched—are hungry for meaningful encounters with God and are eager to be involved in gatherings that encourage a response to their faith. So experiment with these worship services, and adapt them to your own group, its needs, its personality, its students.

How to use
Worship Services for Youth Groups

This book is not intended to necessarily replace your group's worship style, but to complement and perhaps broaden what worship you already have in place. (Unless, of course, you have *no* worship component in your programming, in which case you can use this book to create one.) The beauty of God's creativity is that there is no one, patented way to worship.

Each of these youth worship services is complete—that is, each worship service is made up of components that let the service flow to an appropriate ending. If this or that component just isn't practical for your group, then by all means replace it with something else. Or use the idea merely as a springboard to create a worship element that your students will respond to. What's important is that your students are learning about God and worshipping him authentically and enthusiastically.

Here are a few suggestions for making the most of these twelve worship services, based on my experience with my own youth groups:

+ Be selective in using these services.

This book *isn't* a twelve-week series of worship services. Well, okay—some services *could* be used in a short series—for example, a trinity series on God the Father, God the Son, and God the Holy Spirit (services four, five, and six). In general, though, think of them more as individual services.

Some are designed around the church calendar—Lent (service one in this book), Easter (service two), and Advent (service three)—while others are appropriate for special occasions like baptisms or youth Sundays.

Consider using some of these services at retreats or for special midweek gatherings. Examine each service in light of its potential impact on the lives of your students and plan from there.

+ Familiarize yourself with each service and prepare ahead of time.

For the most part, these services are complete—but that doesn't mean you don't prepare. You just can't wing a worship service. A well-prepared service is a well-received service. And adding your own touches only customizes the service for your own group.

It may be quicker and easier (in the short run) to run a youth meeting by yourself. But these aren't youth meetings—they're youth worship services. That means participation is required if authentic worship will occur. So take time to review the drama, prayers, music, and readings—and do this with students and your volunteers. The time you invest in planning *with them* gives them assurance and confidence as they assist in leading your group in worship.

+ Be open to different worship styles and experiences.

There are a plethora of tastes, styles, and preferences when it comes to worship. There's also much wisdom in acknowledging the validity of many of them, and there's even *more* wisdom in "tasting" some of these styles outside your own tradition.

Some of those styles (common American worship styles, and greatly simplified here):
• *Liturgical* churches tend to be as mystical in their understanding of worship and the sacraments as they are restrained and formal in their worshipping style.
• *Pentecostal* churches are generally also mystical (though in a different way), but in their worship style are freewheeling rather than formal.
• *Fundamentalist* churches are literal rather than mystical, and they're skeptical of both Pentecostal worship (too boisterous) and liturgical worship (too sterile).

• *Charismatic* worship, birthed out of the Jesus movement of twenty-five years ago, sings and strums no-compromise Christian lyrics to a classic rock sound—a sound, by the way, that has influenced worship across most denominations. (This is the sound popularized on Maranatha! and Integrity praise albums.)

• *Evangelicals*, though a little queasy with charismatic theology, recognize the value and appeal of charismatic worship music.

• *Mainline* denominations generally share the evangelicals' queasiness with charismatic theology, but they *are* singing charismatic worship songs (songs, that is, that charismatic churches sang fifteen years ago, and that evangelical churches sang five years ago).

Whatever your style, use some of the ideas in *Worship Services for Youth Groups* as a catalyst to stretch your students and help them appreciate worship practices different from their own. These services have the potential of taking your students out of their comfort zones.

✛ If your youth group isn't a singing group...

Singing has always been a big part of worship, pagan or Christian. Yet some youth groups simply don't sing, for any number of reasons—no leaders, no tradition or model for worship singing, too small a group to think they can sing effectively, no accompanist.

The obvious solution, of course, is to get—or hire, or pray in—an accompanist or leader. Or start with "nonsinging" songs—choral readings, for example, to be done at first, perhaps, for performance purposes (as opposed to celebrative or devotional purposes), to start your meetings or even as the call to worship in your main morning service. Choral readings fit *any* style worship service. (Service five in this book contains a simple choral reading.)

Or join groups or gatherings whose kids have a singing tradition. Interesting things can transpire during such occasions besides exposure to kids who like to sing. Don was an off-and-on volunteer youth worker who happened to join a denominational high school winter retreat. He also happened to be an experienced guitar-playing song leader. Talking around with several youth ministers during the weekend, he discovered that most of the youth groups at the retreat sang only twice a year—summer camp and winter retreat—because their youth ministers couldn't sing, couldn't lead singing, or couldn't accompany—and couldn't snag someone in their congregations to do it.

So Don loaned himself out on Wednesday nights to one of the groups, for whom he led a half-hour of singing each week—and shared his song sheets and chord charts with two or three beginning guitar players in that group. The gig lasted a few months. A year later he hooked up with another group with the same need. Don doesn't know if anyone stepped in after he left these groups, "but at least the kids got a taste of regular, weekly singing together as a group."

✛ Estimate your time.

Most of these services will take about an hour; some a little more, some a little less. Since each youth group meeting time varies, make the necessary adjustments to fit your particular situation. By all means, kill some of the material if you must to make it fit your time frame. Pare them too much, though, and the services begin losing their effectiveness. Sometimes it takes a while to get in a worshipping mind-set—and once there, you don't want to rush out of it.

✛ Adapt a service to your particular group size and room situation.

Don't give up on a service just because you think it won't work with the size of your group. With just a little creativity, each of these services can work well with a group of any size.

Don't forget your room, either—lighting, staging, seating, multimedia, and sound. Do what you can to create the best environment for each service. In some cases, the effect of a service is heightened by meeting somewhere besides your regular youth room.

✦ Be flexible.

Because these services are designed to steer students into direct interaction with God, you'll likely encounter situations where hurts, struggles, needs, and joy are brought to the surface. Your teenagers may want to speak with you or a volunteer in a personal ministry time.

So be flexible and adapt to the immediate needs of your students. Don't be tied to the order of the service if you feel God is leading otherwise. The purpose of these services is for God to work in your students, and for them to respond to him. If that is accomplished without finishing the service as this book or you have outlined it, so be it.

✦ Remember that worship is more than mere programming.

It may be the most (or the only) direct, intimate time with God your kids have all week. I know (as you may) what it's like being so busy that I just throw youth meetings together, because I have to have "something" ready.

Try to slow down and take your time with these services. Commit each aspect of the service to God. Ask him to lead *through* you as you minister to your students. Ask parents to pray, wherever they are during the time the services occur. And check your own heart, too, before you lead others in worship. Then trust God to work, visibly and invisibly, in your group's teenagers.

A word about some helpful features in this book:

Every so often you'll see text that looks like this—in boldface, and with that dark vertical swash there in the margin. These are suggested comments for you (or for whoever leads the worship service) to read verbatim to the students. Of course, you can improvise as much as you want.

Finally, in the back of the book (beginning on page 91) are lists of all the songs and videos used in these worship services, indexed according to the services they're used in, and complete with all the information you need to find and order them.

STANDING AT THE FOOT OF THE CROSS

Remembering Good Friday and the crucifixion

Overview

We worship Christ because he died for us. This service is designed to bring your students to the foot of the Cross so they can come away having seen and understood Christ's unparalleled sacrifice and unconditional love for them. The service will capture the imagination of your students through use of video, narration, music, meditation, confession, and the physical act of nailing their sins to a cross.

Elements of worship

• Student-led opening prayer
• Introductory devotional thoughts
• Focus on the Cross (video or narration option)
• Devotional thoughts
• Special music/personal reflection (writing/confessing sins)
• Praise and worship/personal response (nailing sins to a cross)
• Closing prayer
• Closing praise (optional)

Volunteers needed

• Student to lead opening prayer
• Soloist or ensemble for special music (optional)
• Adult leader to close in prayer

Room preparation

Your room might normally be raucous and bright during a typical youth meeting. This day, have your room darkened save for a single light (a spotlight, large flashlight, or overhead projector will work) shining on a

Materials checklist

☐ Instrumental music (optional)

☐ Music video "Secret Ambition" (optional)

☐ Material for narration: *The Message* or *Six Hours One Friday* (optional)

☐ Accompaniment track, recording, or music video for special music, "How Can You Say No?"

☐ Music for group worship:
  First set:
  • "As the East Is from the West"
  • "Nothing but the Blood of Jesus"
  • "It's Your Blood"
  • "White as Snow"
  • "Cares Chorus"
  • "All I Need Is You"
  • "Oh, How He Loves You and Me"
  Second set:
  • "Lord, I Lift Your Name on High"
  • "I Believe in Jesus"

☐ Large wooden cross

☐ Horseshoe nails for everyone (available at any tack and feed store)

☐ Mallet or hammer. The horseshoe nails and mallet are suggested for their more biblical appearance, however a modern hammer and nails also work fine. Students will nail pieces of paper to the cross so try the hammer and nails ahead of time to make sure they won't have any trouble.

☐ Paper and pencils for everyone

large, crude wooden cross somewhere in your room. Instrumental music may also help enhance the more somber atmosphere of this meeting. The objective is not to be a downer but for students to seriously contemplate the true meaning of Christ and his sacrifice for them.

Student-led opening prayer
(2 minutes)

Have a student pray that hearts and minds would be focused on Christ, asking that God will give a fresh, real, and personal understanding of his sacrifice on the Cross.

Devotional thoughts
(5 minutes)

The objective here is to have students open their minds afresh to the personal impact of the Cross, despite the fact that it is an utterly familiar account and symbol. Say something like this:

In today's society a cross tends to represent different things to different people. To some a cross may be—
- **a religious symbol**
- **a sign of rebellion**
- **a fashion accessory**
- **a symbol of Christ's sacrifice for sin**

Even for those of you who actually understand that a cross is a symbol of Christ's sacrifice for your sins, the story may be so familiar that you are almost apathetic about it—the most remarkable and profound event in human history. Without the death of Christ and his resurrection there would be no hope for us at all (1 Corinthians 15:14). Open your heart and mind to understand, in a new and deeper way, Christ's unbelievable sacrifice for you.

Focusing on the Cross—video or narration option (5 minutes)

Continue your service with one of the following representations of the actual events of the Cross. During this time simply pass a container with the horseshoe nails and ask the students to take and hold a nail for the remainder of the service (they will be used at the end). The nail is a powerful symbol that will help keep them focused on the Cross.

"Secret Ambition"

Michael W. Smith's video "Secret Ambition" is a powerful musical and visual tool that will keep students' attention riveted on the Cross. Between musical scenes, dramatic footage of Christ's ministry and brutal crucifixion are portrayed.

"Secret Ambition" is from the album, *I 2(Eye)* and featured on the video collection, *Two x 4* available from Reunion Records (1989). A popular youth video, it can be rented or ordered at most Christian bookstores.

Turn the lights down in your room and ask your students to close their eyes and try to picture the story of Christ's death as you read it to them aloud (Matthew 27:27-37, 45-50).

Reading the account from a translation such as *The Message* (trans. Eugene Peterson, published by NavPress) or a book such as Max Lucado's *Six Hours One Friday* (chapter 13, pp. 21-23) may also be very effective because they will present the events in a new light for your students.

More devotional thoughts
(5 minutes)

Having focused on Christ's death on the cross, reemphasize some of the painful details to help make it real to the students (Matthew 27:27-37, 45-50). Trace aloud for them the progress of Christ's passion:

verses 27-29 The guards mocked him by dressing Jesus as a king. His head was pierced by long, sharp thorns. Envision the blood running down his face.

verse 30 They spit upon him, which was the deepest form of insult in the Jewish culture.

verse 32 Jesus was already so weak from his earlier 39 lashes with a cat-o'-nine-tails that he could not even carry his own cross bar.

verse 34 Jesus refused to drink the wine mixed with gall (vinegar) because it was given to numb his senses. Jesus was unwilling to numb the pain of dying.

verse 35 Large spikes were driven through both wrists and feet and hammered deep into the wood of the cross. Christ's body received a painful jolt as the cross fell violently into its hole. With the body stretched out on the cross, the person would usually die of suffocation. Some would last for days on the cross, suffering a terrible death.

The cross was brutal, but what actually put Christ up there?
• The Romans? The Jews? No—we did.
• We deserve death for our sins. We should have been up there, not Christ (Romans 3:23, 6:23).
• Christ loves us so much that he chose to take the punishment for our sins so we could have life forever, not eternal death in hell (Romans 5:8).

Special music/personal reflection
(5 minutes)

"How Can You Say No?" is a beautiful and moving song about Christ's sacrifice at the Cross. Have one of your students, leaders, or a youth ensemble sing this song while students contemplate its message and take time for personal reflection.

Although a live performance of this song has the strongest impact, you may also play the recording and ask students to meditate on the words as they listen. It is also available as a music video on the video collection, *Command Performance* (Myrrh) as well as *Edge TV—Edition 6* (Youth Specialties/NavPress).

During the song ask students to write down a sin or sins with which they are currently struggling. They can write down as much as they want; the papers are anonymous and won't be read. Encourage them to be honest and serious, realizing that it was their sins that took Christ to the Cross, but it was also his sacrifice that cleanses them, prompting a response of gratitude and worship. Have students fold and hold their papers.

Praise and worship/personal response: Nailing our sins to the cross
(20 minutes)

After the special music, move into a time of praise and worship through singing. After the first song, instruct the students to get out of their seats and move forward to the wooden cross you have situated in the room. The students should get up individually, as they feel led, anytime during the singing.

When they get to the cross, one at a time have them take their horseshoe nails and the mallet and physically nail their sins to the cross. When they're done, have them kneel, either at the cross or at their seats, imagining themselves alone at the foot of the cross as Jesus pays the price for their sins. Continue your worship time until all of the students have come forward.

A note on the logistics of this activity: if the orientation of the cross or the number of students are prohibitive, instead of nailing the sins up, simply have the students put their paper on a nail or nails protruding from the cross. The horseshoe nails can still be used and kept by the students as a reminder of Christ's sacrifice.

Here's a list of song suggestions (some old, some new) that deal with the theme of the Cross:
• "As the East Is from the West"
• "Nothing but the Blood of Jesus"
• "It's Your Blood"
• "White as Snow"
• "Cares Chorus"
• "All I Need Is You"
• "Oh, How He Loves You and Me"

Closing prayer
(2 minutes)

Have an adult leader pray, thanking God for Christ's sacrifice, love, and forgiveness.

Closing praise (optional; 2-5 minutes)
An upbeat praise song or two will help your students leave the service focused, but rejoicing:
• "Lord, I Lift Your Name on High"
• "I Believe in Jesus"

THE STARK, STUPENDOUS FACT OF THE RESURRECTION

Responding to the reality of Christ's resurrection

Overview

For many students the Easter Story is so familiar that they have become jaded to its impact and importance. By confronting some of the actual theories offered by those who would try to explain away the resurrection, the miracle of its reality becomes fresh and powerful. Students will be renewed in their appreciation for the miraculous nature of Christ's resurrection. This service uses humorous but thought-provoking dramatic presentations for a fresh approach to the truth of the resurrection of Christ.

Elements of worship

- Scripture reading
- **Resurrection Monologs**
- Special music
- Worship through singing (optional)
- Conclusion
- Closing prayer
- Baptisms (optional)

Volunteers needed

- Three student readers, male or female
- Four actors: Roman guard, female scientist, male chauvinist, and girl. Actors can be students or adults.
- Soloist or ensemble for special music
- Someone to close in prayer

Room preparation

Little room preparation is needed. Just a

Materials checklist

☐ Copies of Scripture readings for the three readers (or they may simply read the passages from their Bibles)

☐ 4 copies of **Resurrection Monologs** (page 23)

☐ Costumes for the four actors

☐ Accompaniment track or recording for special music: "Glory to the Lamb" or "Messiah"

☐ Music for group worship:
- "Lord, I Lift Your Name on High"
- "I Am the Resurrection and the Life"
- "I Believe in Jesus"
- "You Have Broken the Chains"

☐ Baptism needs (optional)

stage, or place up front where the readers and actors will be heard.

Scripture reading
(3-4 minutes)
The service begins with two of the three readers on stage (or up front) together. They each read their parts from 1 Corinthians about the debate over the resurrection. The third reader will come up after the **Resurrection Monologs**.

Reader 1: (1 Corinthians 15:12-14) But if it is preached that Christ has been raised from the dead, how can some of you say that there is no resurrection of the dead? If there is no resurrection of the dead, then not even Christ has been raised. And if Christ has not been raised, our preaching is useless and so is your faith.

Reader 2: (1 Corinthians 15:16-19) For if the dead are not raised, then Christ has not been raised either. And if Christ has not been raised, your faith is futile; you are still in your sins. Then those also who have fallen asleep in Christ are lost. If only for this life we have hope in Christ, we are to be pitied more than all men.
(Readers exit, clearing stage for drama)

Resurrection monologs
(20 minutes)
At this point the monologs are read (pages 23-24). When the actors finish, they immediately exit the stage, and Reader 3 continues:

Scripture reading continued
(2 minutes)
Reader 3: (1 Corinthians 15:20-22) But Christ has indeed been raised from the dead, the first fruits of those who have fallen asleep. For since death came through a man, the resurrection of the dead comes also through a man. For as in Adam all die, so in Christ all will be made alive.

Special music
(5 minutes)
Following the Scripture reading, have students worship and celebrate the reality of the resurrection while the triumphant "Glory to the Lamb" or "Messiah" is sung by a soloist or youth ensemble.

group singing option

Worship through singing (5-15 minutes)
Have students join in worship through singing with the following songs:
• "Lord, I Lift Your Name on High"
• "I Am the Resurrection and the Life"
• "I Believe in Jesus"
• "You Have Broken the Chains"

Depending on your group and on your style, you may want to clarify the arguments presented in the **Resurrection monologs.** Say something like—

There have been lots of theories over the centuries that attempt to explain away the resurrection of Jesus. The voices you just heard represent three of the most common theories—theories that, under scrutiny, fall apart.

Theory 1: the disciples stole the body (presented by the Roman guard).
This theory is actually the original cover-up contrived by the chief priests at the time of Jesus' crucifixion, as they conspired with the Roman guards to hide the fact that Jesus was indeed supernaturally resurrected.

Read the account in Matthew 28:11-15.
Refutations of the theory:
First, for the disciples to have stolen the body, the guards would have to have been asleep—which is virtually impossible, considering that Roman soldiers were typically executed for falling asleep on watch. Besides, how could they have not heard the disciples levering the stone from the tomb door?

Second, the disciples themselves never anticipated that Jesus was to be resurrected—hence, their depression the night of the crucifixion. They thought that it was all over. So why would they try to fake a resurrection they never anticipated in the first place?

Third, if the disciples stole the body, faked a "resurrection," and then spread the word that Jesus rose from the dead—why did almost all of the disciples die a martyr's death? It's just plain stupid to die for what one knows is a hoax.

Theory 2: Jesus didn't die, he merely passed out from the pain of the crucifixion (presented by the scientist).
Then later, the theory goes, the cool of the tomb and the pungent aroma of the burial spices revived him. Jesus apparently got up, unwrapped himself, pushed away the stone, rendered the Roman guards helpless, appeared to the disciples, and was never heard from again.

Refutation of the theory:
First, four Roman executioners could not all have been mistaken about whether Jesus was actually dead or no. Killing was their line of work, and they were professionals.

Second, John 19:34 states that blood and water flowed out from his side where the guard's spear pierced him. Blood loss alone would have been enough to kill Jesus.

Third, a man who had been through the torture of crucifixion (not to mention the preliminary flogging by Herod's soldiers) could not have unwrapped his burial wrappings (heavy from many pounds of spices), moved a heavy stone, overpowered several professional soldiers—and still have looked alive enough to support a claim of divine resurrection to his disciples.

Theory 3: the women went to the wrong tomb (presented by the male chauvinist).
After all, the theory claims, it *was* before dawn. In the darkness they took a wrong turn—then convinced themselves that, whoever it was they saw (the gardener perhaps?) was the resurrected Jesus.

Read Luke 24:1-11.
Refutation of the theory:
First, it was an angel that pointed out the tomb to the women. So when was the last time an angel made that kind of mistake?

Second, Peter and John must have gone to the wrong tomb, too—a highly coincidental mistake. Too high, in fact, to be realistic.

Third, all the chief priests would have had to do to quash the cult right then and there was to simply go to the correct tomb, produce the body, and that would've been that. The claims of Jesus' followers about a resurrection would have been exposed as false. But the priests didn't do this.

Conclusion: Jesus was resurrected from the dead as he predicted (in Luke 18:31-34, for example).

Among many good books that explore sound and logical arguments for the resurrection of Christ, see *Who Moved the Stone?* by Frank Morison (Zondervan, 1958—yes, it's an oldie, but it's still a goodie). Josh McDowell's *Evidence That Demands a Verdict* and John Stott's *Basic Christianity* appeared a decade or so later and articulate evidences for the resurrection. Great source material for youth talks.

Conclusion
(2 minutes)

After the special music or worship time have the youth pastor or adult leader conclude the service with the following comments about the remarkable life and death of Christ:

If God were to become a human, what would you expect?
- **He would have a unique and miraculous entrance into the world.**
- **He would live a sinless life.**
- **His words would be authoritative, profound, and true.**
- **He would manifest supernatural powers.**
- **He would make a permanent and irreversible impact on the world and the lives of men.**
- **He would have power over death.**
    God did become a man—and his name was Jesus!

Closing prayer

Worship God through prayer for the miracle of his resurrection and our own eternal life. Give the students some time to pray either silently or out loud before having someone close.

Baptism service

Another appropriate way to end this service of worship on the resurrection is to move together to a location where the group can celebrate in a baptism service for some of your students. Baptism is the ultimate celebration and symbol of the power of Christ's resurrection to transform lives.

Resurrection Monologs

ROMAN GUARD

(As he walks onto the stage, he's nodding his head with a mocking laugh)
Right. If Christ wasn't raised from the dead, then the Christians are to be pitied more than all men. Pity...I'd agree with that. Those weak, pathetic little Christ-followers, putting all their hope in a <u>dead</u> leader. Sure, if Christ were actually resurrected, actually sat up in his tomb and walked out—now <u>that'd</u> be something.

But I'll tell you what really happened.

Those disciples of his, they knew right where the tomb was. And when everyone had gone home, they snuck in and stole the body of Christ. Then *(sarcastically)* <u>miracle of miracles</u>, they announced that Christ had "resurrected." Of course we couldn't find the body. <u>They</u> had it! Pretty soon, they had everyone believing it. As a matter of fact, some people even think they <u>saw</u> Christ after the resurrection. Obviously, delusions.

But just the same, I wouldn't have wanted to be those guys who were supposed to be guarding the tomb. I watched them get run through with swords, the whole bunch of them. Oh well, I guess that's what they get for not guarding their post. Anyway, this "resurrection" thing is just a bunch of stories.

(A female scientist walks onto the stage, joining the Roman guard and speaking to the audience with an air of intellectual confidence)

SCIENTIST

Well, I appreciate the <u>so-called</u> theory of this overgrown boy scout. But if the disciples stole the body, then why didn't anyone ever confess? After all, each and every one of them was repeatedly imprisoned, tortured, and finally killed in horrible ways. Very few men are willing to die for the truth, but why would these twelve men all die for what they knew to be a lie? It makes no sense.

What actually happened is this: Jesus didn't actually die on the cross, you see. He merely passed out. After all, there is no debate about the cruelty of his beatings. I'm sure he lost a great deal of blood and, after hanging on the cross for a day, getting very little oxygen, he passed out, perhaps even slipping into a coma. Then, when he was prepared for burial and lay in the grave, the aromatic spices and cold temperature revived him. He simply unwrapped the burial cloth, pushed away the stone, and walked out. That is the clinical and factual truth of the so-called "resurrection." Case closed.

(Enter an arrogant, obnoxious male chauvinist, either modern-day or period, who joins the two already on stage)

MALE CHAUVINIST

I hate to contradict such an obviously well-educated young lady, but there are a few holes in her theory. First of all, she neglected the fact that when the soldiers thrust a sword into the dead body of Christ both blood and "water" came out. That means that the blood and plasma had separated, which only happens after death. Also, she is also obviously unfamiliar with Jewish burial practices. More than a hundred pounds of spices are wrapped in layer upon layer of tightly wound cloth strips around the body. The result is basically what the Egyptians call a mummy. Trust me—if the cross didn't kill him, the burial would have! And, incidentally, the stone in front of the tomb would have required several grown men and a lever to move it. No half-dead man could have even budged it.

This is what really happened: the women who claimed that they found the tomb empty simply went to the wrong tomb. Now remember, these were silly women, prone to fits of emotion. They were probably up all night crying. They were tired, their eyes were probably all puffy and red, and it was dark outside. In their typical female confusion they went to the wrong tomb and, seeing it empty, began their hysterical rantings about some so-called resurrection. No mystery here, just an understandable case of female error.

(A young girl enters and addresses the chauvinist)

GIRL

Excuse me?

MALE CHAUVINIST

Yes, little girl?

GIRL

If the women went to the wrong tomb, why didn't either the Jews or the Romans simply find the right tomb and produce the body of Christ?

MALE CHAUVINIST

Well, I...you see...uh...

GIRL

And didn't an angel of God speak to them and show them the tomb? Was the angel confused, too?

MALE CHAUVINIST

Well, I don't know about any angel...uh...

GIRL

And if Christ wasn't resurrected, how do you explain the more than 500 witnesses who all claim to have seen him after the resurrection? *(Male chauvinist opens his mouth to speak but says nothing)* Just what I thought. In other words, there is no real evidence to support any conclusion except that Christ was actually resurrected from the dead. Thank you very much.

(All exit)

THE MEANING OF THE MANGER

A personal response to Christ's birth

Overview

This creative worship service will lead students progressively deeper into a personal response to the birth of Christ. By seeing the responses of randomly selected individuals (on video), Bible characters (through drama), and then finally their own responses through prayer and meditation, the familiar Christmas story becomes fresh, with a powerful impact to change their lives and the lives of others.

Elements of worship

• Worship God through music—Christmas carols
• Opening prayer
• Special music and/or worship dance
• Student-produced video (optional)
• **Nativity Monologs**—by students or leaders, that retell the Christmas story from four perspectives
• Silent reflection
• Closing prayer and worship

Volunteers needed

• Student to lead opening prayer
• Soloist or ensemble for special music
• Dancers (optional)
• Students to produce video (optional)
• Four actors, three male and one female
• Student or adult reader for Scripture readings

Room preparation

The only special set up you'll need will be during the drama. Dim the lights and use some kind of spotlight to enhance the drama and seriousness of the presentation. Before each vignette have a student or leader read the

Materials checklist

☐ Music for group carols:
  First set
  • "Hark, the Herald Angels Sing"
  • "Joy to the World"
  • "O Come, All Ye Faithful"
  Second set
  • "O Little Town of Bethlehem"
  • "What Child Is This?"
  • "Emmanuel"
  Third set
  • "Away in a Manger"
  • "More Precious Than Silver"
  Fourth set
  • "Silent Night"

☐ Accompaniment track or recording for special music, "The Breath of Heaven (Mary's Song)"

☐ Student-produced video (optional). Send some students or leaders out into a mall or park and videotape the responses of several people to the question, "What does Christmas mean to you?" Be creative and choose a variety of people to interview. Here are some suggestions:
  • three-year-old child
  • senior citizen (80+)
  • policeman
  • teacher or coach
  • local merchant
  • students
  • people shopping
  • shopping-mall Santa

☐ Copies of **Nativity monologs** for actors (pages 28-31)

☐ Biblical costumes for Joseph, Mary, King Herod, and Simeon

indicated passage of Scripture either from up front or on an offstage microphone.

Worship through singing—Christmas carols
(5 minutes)

Begin your service with a time of worship through singing. Traditional carols create a Christmasy atmosphere and prepare the students for what they will be experiencing. Try using contemporary arrangements or accompaniment to give these traditional carols a fresh feel:
• "Hark, the Herald Angels Sing"
• "Joy to the World"
• "O Come, All Ye Faithful"

Opening Prayer
(2 minutes)

Have a student lead an opening prayer thanking God for the gift of his son and inviting the Holy Spirit to open hearts anew to the power and impact of the fact that God came and lived with us here on earth.

Special music/worship dance
(5 minutes)

"The Breath of Heaven (Mary's Song)" is a beautiful song which communicates Mary's humility and dependence on God during the time of Christ's birth. Have a student or leader sing this song for your group. The song could also be enacted through worship dance/movement while it is sung or played. Encourage the students to carefully consider the lyrics to the song and have them try to imagine Mary's thoughts and emotions.

video option
(5 minutes)

In place of or in addition to the special music, play your "What Does Christmas Mean to You?" video.

Nativity monologs
(20 minutes)

Through the video your students have heard the responses of others regarding the meaning of Christmas. Now, through drama, take them back in time to the actual birth of Christ and hear the response of those who were there. Select four strong actors (students or adults) to present the possible remarks of Joseph, Mary, King Herod, and Simeon about the birth of Christ (scripts on pages 28-31). Although fictionalized and humorous, these vignettes are also pointed in their message. Each scene is prefaced by a Scripture reading, read from up front or on an offstage microphone.

Introduction:

We've seen what the world has to say about the birth of Christ, but what impact did his birth have on the people who were there? Let yourself be

transported back in time and be impacted in a fresh way by the news of Christ's birth.

Order of readings and dramatic vignettes:
• Reading of Matthew 1:18-21
• Joseph script (page 28)
• Reading of Luke 1:26-35
• Mary script (page 29)
• Reading Matthew 2:1-8
• Herod script (page 30)
• Reading of Luke 2:21-35
• Simeon script (page 31)

Silent reflection
(3-4 minutes)

The worship service now moves from the responses of others regarding Christ's birth to a time of personal reflection for your students. Keep the lights down in your room to help your students enter a time of worshipful reflection and meditation.

How have *you* responded to Christ's birth this Advent season?

• By making a list of things you want from others?
• By watching "Rudolph the Red-nosed Reindeer?"
• By over-eating?
• Or have you responded by falling at the feet of God in worship for the most amazing, miraculous, and unselfish gift you will ever receive; his own son Jesus Christ. Take the time now to put Christ in your Christmas! Some of you may also want to consider some kind of tangible, personal, or spiritual gift you can give as a worship response to God's ultimate gift for you.

Closing prayer and worship
(10-15 minutes)

Suggestions for interwoven worship songs and prayer.

Songs: "O Little Town of Bethlehem"
        "What Child Is This?"
        "Emmanuel"

Prayer: Invite students to pray aloud, thanking God for the birth of his son and for everything it means to them.

Songs: "Away in a Manger"
        "More Precious Than Silver"

Prayer: Again ask students to pray aloud. Encourage them to pray that God will use them to share the true message of Christmas with an unsaved friend or relative.

Closing song: "Silent Night"

JOSEPH

You know, I've been checking out the woodwork you've got around here...**(nods his head momentarily, as if looking around)**...Shabby. Too much drywall and plastic for me. But then, I'm a wood man myself. Carpenter by trade. Oh, let me introduce myself. Joseph's the name. Yeah, I used to be pretty well-known for my trade, but of course, I'm known for something else now.

You see, my son—well, I guess, stepson—is Jesus of Nazareth. I say stepson because though I raised him as my own, his natural father is Jehovah himself.

Sure, it's easy to talk about it now. But at the time it really took some getting used to. You see Mary and I were engaged and I was pretty excited about it. You know, with it being an arranged marriage I was prepared for the worst, but when I saw her...wow! And when I started to get to know her...it was even better! She was sweet, pure, godly, and she really had a great sense of humor, too.

As a matter of fact, I thought it was a joke when she told me, just a few months before our wedding, that she was pregnant. "Yeah, right!," I said, "and the Rabbi eats ham!" **(laughs)** But then I looked at her and I knew in an instant that this was no joke. The tears filled her eyes as my anger and outrage burned. "You're <u>what</u>!" I yelled. "Who's the father? I can't believe you! I mean, what are you, some kind of whore?"

It was only her quiet sobs that made me calm down enough to finally listen. There she was, this tender girl. The girl I loved. She told me that she was still a virgin, that she was pregnant by the Holy Spirit and that an angel had told her that she would give birth to the Messiah, the son of God.

I listened to her story but I have to admit, when I left her that day I was still fairly sure that she was either a liar or just plain crazy. I cared about her, but I still didn't know what to do. It wasn't until I was also visited by an angel that I began to understand. The angels said that what Mary had told me was all true. She was carrying the son of the Most High God and I...**(tenderly)**...I was going to be his daddy.

Well you know the story from there. You know, I didn't plan any of it, but looking back now I see that it all happened according to the prophecies and God's plan. And I guess that's the story of how my son became my Lord.

(Looking up) Jehovah...Thanks for letting me get to know your boy...he's a great kid.

MARY

You know, maybe today this teen pregnancy thing is no big deal, but trust me, you'd have a lot fewer of them today if you had rules like we had. Under Jewish law, if you were unfaithful to your fiancee you would be publicly disgraced, stripped naked, and hit with stones until you were dead. That's a pretty strong case for abstinence if you ask me.

That's why I was pretty shook up when an angel came to me and told me that I was going to be pregnant. Of course my first thoughts were panic, but the angel seemed to know that. He told me not to be afraid because I was going to give birth to the son of God. The Messiah. *(Pause)* You would've thought I'd freak out, but there's nothing I can say that describes the calm that enveloped me.

Don't get me wrong, I never thought that it was going to be easy. First I had to tell Joseph—and boy, did he ever blow up at first. Then there was the morning sickness. . . and then the trip to Bethlehem. *(Sarcastically)* Perfect timing! You know all those pictures of me riding on a donkey into town? Don't you believe it! I walked the <u>whole</u> way and my ankles were *so* swollen! And please, let's not even mention the stable. I smelled like manure for a week! Well, it wasn't great, but you know, I did still have that peace because God was with me.

It seemed like that night would never end. The trip. The filth. The pain! Oh, I prayed to God that it would all just be over. But when Jesus was finally born and I looked into the red, wrinkled, puffy little face of that sweet boy, my prayer became a prayer of praise. I was looking into the eyes of God.

HEROD

Being ruler of Judea used to be a lot of fun. Taxes to collect, prisoners to torture, concubines to...well, you get the picture. But lately it's been a real drag. The Jews have been restless, looking for their "Messiah," their new "king."

Don't they get it? I'm their king. They shall have no other king beside me. I am Herod, ruler over all of Judea.

You may wonder why I'm so worried about this now. Of course, I've heard all the talk, the prophecies about the coming Messiah. But until recently that's all it was, just talk about something that might happen someday. Then yesterday I got a visit that I admit, has made me a little nervous. A huge caravan of royal scientists, astrologers, and rulers from the east arrived. They believe that a star has appeared which marks the birth of the Jewish Messiah. They had traveled hundreds of miles to seek and worship the new king!

What do they care? They're not even Jewish!

Well, needless to say I was pretty upset. I can't believe it may have actually happened. But I'm not about to be displaced by some baby! King indeed. Well, I played it cool. You see, I told them that when they find this tot king, that they should tell me where he is so I can go worship him, too *(sinister laugh; then sarcastically)* Yeah, I'll give him a royal welcome all right...with the edge of a sword!

King of the Jews or not, it's going to take more than a baby to beat old Herod. I mean, who does he think he is? God?!

(Exit muttering...)

Jews!...Why didn't I take that transfer to Decapolis when I had the chance?

SIMEON

You know, we Jews have always had a hard time. Conquered here, enslaved there, in and out of the promised land every couple of generations. There was a lot of suffering. Struggling under the Roman rule; some people were losing hope. It had been so long since the Messiah had been promised. Some were beginning to believe that our deliverer, the promised Christ, would never come.

I was in my room one evening, crying out to God over the sins of our people. I asked him when would Messiah come? As I prayed in my dark room, I must have drifted off to sleep (don't you hate it when that happens?), because suddenly I was awakened by a voice and a light so bright that I was almost blinded. The voice said, "Simeon, Simeon, your faithfulness will be rewarded. I say unto you that you will not pass from this earth until your eyes have seen the promised Messiah."

From that moment on I rejoiced. I was filled with new hope and began to tell everyone that Messiah was near. As the months and years passed, my health began to deteriorate. Yet even old as I was, I went out each day to the temple, waiting and watching for the one who had been promised to me.

Today, as I walked up the steps into the courtyard, I passed through the usual crowd when I saw a poor couple walking in with a baby. It was not an unusual sight; parents often came to the temple with babies to be circumcised or blessed.

I gave this couple no more than a casual glance when a voice spoke to me, "Behold your Messiah."

Slowly I approached the couple. So young. So poor. Could it really be that the promised king would come as a baby from such a family? I had been looking for a king, a ruler, a grown man with authority and power. Not a gurgling, defenseless babe. And yet, when I looked into the face of this baby, God spoke again: "Behold my son." I asked the young couple if I could hold their baby. As the mother handed him to me, she whispered, "His name is Jesus."

"Jesus, Lord Jesus," I said as a I held him. I cried out to all in the temple yard, "Here is our salvation! I can die now in peace because I have seen our promised deliverer."

Well, that's it. That's my story. Since then I've been telling everyone that Messiah has finally come. Many have believed and are rejoicing like me. And though some still doubt, I know they'll see in time. After all, he's not going to be a baby forever.

he People Who Brought You This Book . . .

—invite you to discover MORE valuable youth-ministry resources—

'outh Specialties offers an assortment of books, publications, tapes, and events, all 'esigned to encourage and train youth workers and their kids. Just return this card, nd we'll send you FREE information on our products and services.

Please send me the FREE Youth Specialties Catalog and information on upcoming Youth Specialties events.

you: ❏ A volunteer youth worker (or) ❏ A salaried youth worker   480001

me _____ Title _____

urch/Organization _____

dress: ❏ Home (or) ❏ Church _____

y _____ State _____ Zip _____

ne Number: ❏ Home (or) ❏ Church (_____)_____

Mail address _____

he People Who Brought You This Book . . .

—invite you to discover MORE valuable youth-ministry resources—

'outh Specialties offers an assortment of books, publications, tapes, and events, all 'esigned to encourage and train youth workers and their kids. Just return this card, nd we'll send you FREE information on our products and services.

Please send me the FREE Youth Specialties Catalog and information on upcoming Youth Specialties events.

you: ❏ A volunteer youth worker (or) ❏ A salaried youth worker   480001

me _____ Title _____

urch/Organization _____

dress: ❏ Home (or) ❏ Church _____

y _____ State _____ Zip _____

ne Number: ❏ Home (or) ❏ Church (_____)_____

Mail address _____

Call toll-free to order:
(800) 776-8008

BUSINESS REPLY MAIL
FIRST-CLASS MAIL   PERMIT 268   HOLMES PA

POSTAGE WILL BE PAID BY ADDRESSEE

YOUTH SPECIALTIES
P.O. BOX 668
HOLMES, PA 19043-0668

Call toll-free to order:
(800) 776-8008

NO POSTAG
NECESSARY
IF MAILED
IN THE
UNITED STAT

BUSINESS REPLY MAIL
FIRST-CLASS MAIL   PERMIT 268   HOLMES PA

POSTAGE WILL BE PAID BY ADDRESSEE

YOUTH SPECIALTIES
P.O. BOX 668
HOLMES, PA 19043-0668

HOW BIG IS YOUR GOD?

Discovering the character of God the Father

Overview

All students go through times when they feel that God is impersonal and uninvolved in their lives. This worship service focuses on God the Father and is designed to reveal the character of God, to help students understand that he is both big and personal. When students gain a deeper understanding of who God is, it can only prompt a worshipful response. This service uses a creative object lesson throughout, as well as prayer, and a unique worship time which includes the giving of a "gift of obedience" as an act of worship to God.

Elements of worship

Students will be drawn into a worship experience focused on the person and character of God as they respond and interact with the service elements:
• Praise and worship
• Scriptural call to worship
• Student-led opening prayer
• Student-produced video interviews
• Creative student prayer time
• What God says about it
• Spiritual allegory
• Worship through music and a "gift of obedience"
• Play-dough object lesson

Volunteers needed

• Student to read passage of Scripture and say an opening prayer
• Students or staff members to produce a video of interviews
• Two adult leaders to read passages of Scripture

Materials checklist

☐ Music for group worship:
   First set
   • "You Are the Mighty King"
   • "Almighty"
   • "Awesome God"
   • "Holy, Holy, Holy"
   • "How Great Thou Art"
   • "Abba Father" (The Family Song)
   Second set
   • "I Stand in Awe"
   • "Great Is the Lord"

☐ Video interviews. During the week prior to the service either you, a staff member, or students go out into the community (a mall or busy entertainment areas are good possibilities) and videotape the responses of five to ten people to the following question: "How or to what extent is God involved in your life?" You're sure to get a variety of responses.

☐ Copies of **Anonymous Prayer cards** and **My Gift to God cards** for all students (page 38)

☐ Prepare a large Gift for God box. It should be wrapped like an elegant gift, with a slot cut for the **My Gift to God cards**.

☐ Pencils for everyone.

☐ Make up enough play dough (recipe on page 34) so that each person can have a small handful. You may also use commercial Play Doh or clay.

RECIPE FOR PLAY DOUGH

Makes enough for about 25 people to have a small ball. Double or triple the batch as the need dictates.

    1 cup flour
    2 tsp. cream of tartar
    ½ cup salt
    1 T. cooking oil
    1 cup water
    1 pkg. unsweetened Kool-Aid

Mix dry ingredients in a saucepan or pot. Add oil, water, and Kool-Aid (dry). Cook for five minutes on medium heat or until the mixture pulls away from the pan. Stir constantly. Cool slightly and knead to smooth consistency and even coloring.

Looks and feels like commercial Play Doh and smells great—and is nontoxic. Keeps indefinitely without refrigeration in an airtight container.

Room preparation

Place a small piece of clay, commercial Play Doh, or homemade play dough (see recipe, this page) on each person's chair. Don't tell students what the clay is for; just let them fiddle with it throughout the service. The clay is actually an object lesson, whose purpose will be highlighted at the end of the service.

Each chair should also have an **Anonymous Prayer card**, a **My Gift to God card** (both on page 38), and a pencil.

✦　✦　✦　✦　✦　✦　✦

Praise and worship
(15 minutes)

Begin the service with a time of singing praise to the Lord. Share with your students that the focus of the service is God the Father; who he is and what he's like. Encourage them to begin considering who God really is to them. The following is a list of song suggestions (some new, some old) that describe God's character:
• "You Are the Mighty King"
• "Almighty"
• "Awesome God"
• "Holy, Holy, Holy"
• "How Great Thou Art"
• "Abba Father" (The Family Song)

Call to worship
(5 minutes)

Immediately following the singing, have a student stand and read Psalm 139:1-3, 13-16. The Psalm describes God both as our maker and as someone who is deeply concerned about each of us in a personal way. Have the student pray after reading the Scripture, recognizing the qualities of God and thanking him for creating each of us in wonderful and unique ways.

Video opener
(5 minutes)

Introduce and show the edited videotape of responses to the question: "To what extent (or how) is God involved in your life?"

An anonymous prayer
(5-7 minutes)

Tell your students that now it's *their* time to be honest before God about the state of their relationships with him. Have students respond to one or both of the statements on the **Anonymous Prayer card**.

Give the students a few minutes to write their responses and pass in the cards. Redistribute the cards and give the students several minutes to pray for the anonymous person whose praise and/or need is shared on the card they received. You may want to have the lights dimmed and/or have a praise song playing in the background during the distribution/prayer time.

What God says about it
(15 minutes)

Is God the Father *real* to your students? What are their ideas about him? Is he relevant enough to handle their problems? The following brief message is designed to encourage your students by introducing them to two aspects of God's character.

Introduction
If we really understood how big God is, it would change the way we live and relate to him, wouldn't it? Open your mind to God this morning. Let's push out the walls of our imagination and get a fresh look at who God really is.

Share with your students this insight from Walter Henrichsen dealing with our concepts of God—from his book, *Disciples Are Made and Not Born* (Scripture Press, 1974):

Every problem a person has is related to his concept of God. If you have a big God, you have small problems. If you have a small God, you have big problems. It is as simple as that. When your God is big, then every seeming problem becomes an opportunity. When your God is small, every problem becomes an obstacle.

Quality 1: God is big
An Allegory: The Palace of the King
Ask your students to close their eyes and envision themselves in the story as you read it to them.

The palace rises up out of the forested hills like a glacier from the sea. It is a harsh and turbulent bygone era of warriors and rulers. However, the most feared and venerated of all is the great king. He has conquered continents and has just returned from a long and victorious campaign. The city surrounding the palace bears his majestic image in monuments, statues, and great buildings all erected to his glory. Most people are not even allowed to step through the great gated wall that surrounds the royal estates. The most privileged may enter the guarded and grand palace itself, but even they quake in awe of its majesty and splendor. Only a small and select number dare come into the royal court, into the company of the king, and then only by invitation. An uninvited visitor could be killed on the spot for entering his glorious presence.
The crowd in the village parts as you walk toward the palace gate. The people murmur when you pass, wondering how and why you are so privileged to enter the royal grounds. When the armored guards see you, they step aside to allow your passage through the mighty entrance into the palace itself. Royal attendants bow in reverence as you approach the mighty throne room of the

monarch. They tremble in fear as they see you actually reaching for the latch, opening the door to the king's own inner chamber. You walk boldly into the throne room, not in fear, but with honor and respect, bowing reverently at the feet of the almighty king, the conquering warrior, the terrible and fearful ruler...and your *father*.

As soon as you've finished reading the allegory, have two adult leaders prepared to each read one of the following passages while the students continue to meditate. The passages communicate the glory, might, power, and holiness of God:
• Jeremiah 51:15-19
• Revelation 4:1-11

Quality 2: God is personal

Because God is so awesome, it is even more humbling and profound that we can actually know him in a personal way. What's more amazing is that he wants to know us.
　　God has revealed himself to us throughout time:
• **He walked with Adam in the Garden of Eden (Genesis 3:8).**
• **He told Moses his name, Yahweh, which means I AM (Exodus 3:14).**
• **He touched us directly through Jesus, whose name Immanuel means** *God with us* **(Matthew 1:23).**
• **He created us in his image (Genesis 1:27).**
• **He wants us to know him (Jeremiah 9:23-24).**
• **He knows all the days of our lives in detail (Psalm 139:16).**
• **He even knows how many hairs are on our head (Matthew 10:30).**
　　Sometimes we struggle with relating to a God we cannot see, hear, or touch, but that doesn't mean he's not there for us. We can't see the air, but who would question the power of a tornado? I can't see electricity, but I'm not going to put my finger in a light socket!
　　Remember that God the Father has taken the first step to know you as his child and that he promises that if we draw near to him, he will draw near to us (James 4:8). It is not enough to know about God, we must go deeper and experience him personally. How do we get to know him? By talking to him, reading his words to us, being with his people, and doing the things he tells us to do. Then we will not just know about him, but know him intimately, the way we know ourselves, our family, or our closest friends. The more you know God, the bigger you will realize he is; big enough to handle your concerns, questions, and future.

God the Father is seeking to know you. Are you seeking to really know him?

Worship through a gift of obedience
(5-10 minutes)

It's incredible to think about a God that is so powerful, yet so loving. Allow students an opportunity to respond by worshiping God for just who he is. This worship will take place in two ways:

• Worship through music
Sing two (or more as needed) choruses that deal with the greatness of God. Encourage the students to celebrate their wonderful God and the relationship they

can have with him.
▶"I Stand in Awe"
▶"Great Is the Lord"

• *Worship with a gift of obedience*
In the Old Testament worshipers would bring a sacrifice or gift of animals, money, a costly possession, or burnt incense in worship to God. However, 1 Samuel 15:22 and Romans 12:1 say that God desires our obedience and our holy lives more than gifts or sacrifices. During the singing ask your students to reflect and ask God what kind of gift of obedience they could give to him as an act of worship. Here are some suggestions:

- **Forgive someone who has hurt you (Ephesians 4:32).**
- **Be obedient to your parents in a particular area (Ephesians 6:1-3).**
- **End a relationship that is sexually immoral (1 Thessalonians 4:3).**
- **Begin giving a portion of your wages to the Lord's work (2 Corinthians 9:6-7).**
- **Give God your mouth (stop gossiping, 2 Corinthians 12:20; stop cursing, Ephesians 5:4).**
- **Begin a daily time of prayer (Philippians 4:6).**

Have the students use the **My Gift to God cards** to record what they're giving as "gifts of obedience." Ask them to sign and date the cards to help solidify their commitments.

As the students finish their "gift" cards (during the worship), have them come up to the front and deposit them in the elegantly wrapped Gift for God box.

Object lesson
(2 minutes)
To close your service bring your students' attention to the clay most of them have been squeezing and shaping throughout the service. Share with them Isaiah 64:8 which describes God the Father as the potter and us as the clay. Remind them that God, whether overtly or subtly, is constantly at work shaping our lives for his glory. The clay may not see or understand what it will become in the potter's hands, yet it yields. We need to trust in God, in his love for us, and continually yield our lives to him.

Anonymous Prayer

- In what way has God been real to you recently?

- What have you been struggling with recently in your relationship with God?

Anonymous Prayer

- In what way has God been real to you recently?

- What have you been struggling with recently in your relationship with God?

My gift to God is—

_____ (signature)

_____ (date)

My gift to God is—

_____ (signature)

_____ (date)

LIKE FATHER, LIKE SON

The I AM's of Christ

Overview

People have many different ideas about who Jesus really was. Some say he was a prophet; others claim he was crazy or deluded. And there are those who simply don't care. In most secular classes on biblical literature, Jesus is presented as an admirable moral teacher, but certainly nothing more. And then there are those of us who believe he was and is the Son of God and worship him as Savior.

What do your students believe about who Jesus is? Some might perceive him as a rule-giver whose teachings tend to take away their fun. Others might be confused about how he could claim to be both God and man at the same time.

The goal of this service is to deepen your students' understanding about the person of Christ in terms of who *he* said he was. Students have the opportunity to respond to Jesus using a number of unique worship elements, including art, written prayers, choral reading, singing, and a reading meditation.

Elements of worship

The elements below are designed to challenge your students to reconsider their perceptions of Jesus as they worship in a variety of creative ways.
• "Popcorn"-type prayer
• Praise and worship through singing
• Thought-provoking videos about the world's perspective on Christ (optional)
• Choral reading
• Creative artistic expression
• What God says about it
• Student-produced video interviews
• Reading of "**Ragman**," a modern analogy of Christ
• Written prayer to Jesus

Materials checklist

☐ Music for group worship:
  • "I Am the Resurrection and the Life"
  • "You Are the Vine"
  • "Lion and the Lamb"
  • "You Are the Mighty King"
  • "Jesus, Name above All Names"
  • "Jesus Mighty God"
  • "Jesus, What a Wonder You Are"
  • "I Believe in Jesus"
  • "There Is a Redeemer"

☐ Copies of the videos *Jesus* or *Witness* (optional)

☐ Copies of the choral reading I AM for three readers (page 43)

☐ Copy of story **Ragman** (page 44)

☐ Enough paper for everyone to draw on (white card stock works well)

☐ An assortment of pencils and markers and/or collage materials, magazines, and glue

☐ Video interviews. Prior to your service, send a group of students into your community (mall, schools, streets, recreational areas) with a video camera to tape the responses of various people to the question, "Who is Jesus?" Aim for a two-to-four-minute edited video.

☐ A basket of dinner rolls, one for everyone (optional)

Volunteers needed

- Student to explain and open in "Popcorn"-type prayer
- Three readers, either male or female, for the choral reading
- Students or staff members to produce a video of interviews
- An adult or two available afterwards for students who would like to talk or pray

Opening prayer
(5 minutes)

Have a student open your service with a time of group prayer. The student should inform the group that the focus of the morning will be on the claims Christ made about himself. The group will be invited to participate in praying out loud together as they share one-word "popcorn"-type prayers which describe the person of Christ to them.

For example, the leader might start off by saying, "Savior." Then, either randomly or in rows, have students share their prayers ("Friend...Healer...Forgiver," etc.). You may have them hold hands both for unity and so that a student who doesn't want to pray can squeeze the hand of the person next to them to pass.

Praise and worship
(10-15 minutes)

Song suggestions that focus on the person and ministry of Christ:
- "I Am the Resurrection and the Life"
- "You Are the Vine"
- "Lion and the Lamb"
- "You Are the Mighty King"
- "Jesus, Name above All Names"
- "Jesus Mighty God"
- "Jesus, What a Wonder You Are"
- "I Believe in Jesus"
- "There Is a Redeemer"

video option
(5 minutes)

In addition to, or in place of, a time of worship through singing, use a short segment from one of the following videos to help focus your students on who Jesus really was.
- In *Witness* actor Curt Cloninger portrays various characters who knew Jesus. Show a segment you feel will speak best to your students. (Order from Youth Specialties by calling 800/776-8008.)
- Show a segment from *Jesus* by Campus Crusade for Christ. It's available at most Christian bookstores or can be ordered directly from Campus Crusade for Christ, 2700 Little Mountain Dr., P.O. Box 6046, San Bernardino, CA 92412

Choral reading
(5 minutes)

Transition from the praise and worship and/or the video into the choral reading I AM (page 43), which recites the claims Christ made about himself.

A creative worship response
(10-20 minutes)

Many of us stopped using our creative artistic abilities at church about the time we stopped attending vacation Bible school. God has gifted us to express ourselves in a variety of ways.

During this segment of the service, encourage your students to use their imaginations and their artistic abilities (of whatever skill) to worship Jesus through a piece of art they create. Paper and art supplies should be readily available so as not to disrupt the mood of worship.

Suggest they consider the I AM's of Christ mentioned in the choral reading as a possible theme for their work. Their picture can be a representation of Christ, or some kind of depiction of what he means to them.

Students should not talk during this time, since it is an act of worship. You may wish to play some praise music in the background as students draw.

option

When students have completed their works of "worship art," ask a few of them to share with the group.

What God says about it
(15-20 minutes)

Following the art, transition into a brief teaching time, highlighting several of the claims Christ made about himself. A brief outline is given here. Dig deeper as the needs of your students dictate.

Introduction: video "Who Is Jesus?"
Introduce and play the "Who Is Jesus?" video produced by your students the week before.

Teaching: the I AM's of Christ
Transition from video with words to this effect:

It's obvious that people have very different ideas about who Jesus was. But really, the best and most accurate statements are those Jesus made about himself. By studying the I AM's of Christ, we can come to understand him. Let's focus on three of them today.

1. "I am the bread of life."
   Read John 6:25-35.

option

Before you read the passage, pass around a basket full of good fresh rolls. (This isn't communion, just food.) Have the students take one and eat it while you read the passage and discuss Jesus as the Bread of Life.

Jesus was disappointed with the crowd because they were following him only to be physically nourished. They were seeking something else, other than Christ alone to satisfy them. Jesus is the Bread of Life that eternally satisfies those who seek him and put their trust in him (verses 26-27).

Ask your students what satisfies them. Being totally honest, they'd probably say their friends, entertainment, social status, shopping—many things *other* than Jesus.

Explore with your students what it means to be totally satisfied by Jesus.

2. "I am gentle and humble in heart."

Read Matthew 11:28-30.

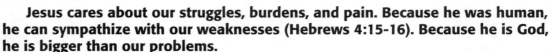

Jesus cares about our struggles, burdens, and pain. Because he was human, he can sympathize with our weaknesses (Hebrews 4:15-16). Because he is God, he is bigger than our problems.

To help us understand this description of Christ, it is probably best to picture a young mother holding a baby. She has to be gentle and tender because her baby is so fragile and weak. And yet, though she is so much bigger and stronger than her baby, the mother is humble. Denying her own needs and desires, she puts her baby before herself. Can you imagine a mother who sits down to eat while her starving child cries. Or a mother who leaves her child at home alone while she goes out to a party. No, it wouldn't (or shouldn't) happen. A mother's humility means that her child comes first. It's just her nature.

It's Christ's nature, too. He's gentle with us—leading and shaping our lives as we yield them to him. And he's humble, putting our needs first, as he did at the Cross.

Finally, doesn't Christ's gentleness and humility make you want to love and follow him? These qualities are like a magnet, drawing us to him like a tender mother.

3. "I am the Resurrection and the Life"
   Read John 11:25-27.

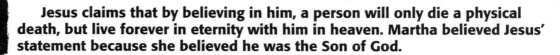

Jesus claims that by believing in him, a person will only die a physical death, but live forever in eternity with him in heaven. Martha believed Jesus' statement because she believed he was the Son of God.

Ask your students if they have the same kind of belief as Martha. Does this faith give assurance about the future? What about the present?

Conclusion

Dim the lights and ask your students to close their eyes as you end by reading them a modern analogy of Christ, **Ragman** by Walter Wangerin, Jr. (page 44-45). The imagery in this story is very powerful and should move your students to consider who Christ really is in terms of his great compassion for us and the salvation that he offers.

Closing—written prayers to Jesus
(5 minutes)

After reading the story, close the service by having students write prayers to Jesus, thanking him for who he is and asking him to work in their lives. Have students write in silence as they focus on their relationships with Jesus. When students are finished, have them leave the room silently. You may wish to have an adult leader or two available for any student who would like to stay after to talk or pray.

I AM

A Choral Reading for Three Readers

(Read with warmth, expression, and growing intensity)

Reader 1:	The Bread of Life
Reader 2:	The Light of the World
Reader 3:	The Good Shepherd
Reader 1:	I Am
Reader 2:	The Teacher
Reader 3:	The Rabbi
Reader 1:	The Son of Man
Reader 2:	I Am
Reader 3:	In the Father and the Father is in me
Reader 1:	I Am
Reader 2:	The True Vine
Reader 3:	The Gate
Reader 1:	The Door
Reader 2:	I Am
Reader 3:	Gentle and humble in heart
Reader 1 & 2:	I Am
Reader 3:	The Lion of the Tribe of Judah
Reader 1:	The Rose of Sharon
Reader 2 & 3:	I Am
Reader 1:	A healer, a servant, a sacrifice
Reader 2 & 3:	I Am
Reader 1:	The Almighty King
Reader 2:	The Righteous Judge
Reader 3:	The Living Word
Reader 1 & 2:	*(building)* I Am
Reader 1:	The Way
Reader 1 & 2:	The Truth
All:	The Life
Reader 1:	I Am
All:	*(louder)* The Resurrection
Reader 1:	I Am
All:	*(louder still)* I Am
All:	*(with quiet intensity)* Jesus

—END—

RAGMAN

by Walter Wangerin, Jr.

Even before the dawn one Friday morning I noticed a young man, handsome and strong, walking the alleys of our City. He was pulling an old cart filled with clothes both bright and new, and he was calling in a clear, tenor voice: "Rags!" Ah, the air was foul, the first light filthy to be crossed by such sweet music.

"Rags! New rags for old! I take your tired old rags! Rags!"

"Now this is a wonder," I thought to myself, for the man stood six-feet-four, and his arms were like tree limbs, hard and muscular, and his eyes flashed intelligence. Could he find no better job than this, to be a ragman in the inner city?

I followed him. My curiosity drove me. And I wasn't disappointed.

Soon the Ragman saw a woman sitting on her back porch. She was sobbing into a handkerchief, sighing, and shedding a thousand tears. Her knees and elbows made a sad X. Her shoulders shook. Her heart was breaking.

The Ragman stopped his cart. Quietly, he walked to the woman, stepping round tin cans, dead toys, and Pampers.

"Give me your rag," he said so gently, "and I'll give you another."

He slipped the handkerchief from her eyes. She looked up, and he laid across her palm a linen cloth so clean and new that it shined. She blinked from the gift to the giver.

Then, as he began to pull his cart again, the Ragman did a strange thing: he put her stained handkerchief to his own face; and then *he* began to weep, to sob as grievously as she had done, his shoulders shaking. Yet she was left without a tear.

"This *is* a wonder," I breathed to myself, and I followed the sobbing Ragman like a child who cannot turn away from mystery.

"Rags! Rags! New rags for old!"

In a little while, when the sky showed grey behind the roof-tops and I could see the shredded curtains hanging out black windows, the Ragman came upon a girl whose head was wrapped in a bandage. A single line of blood ran down her cheek.

Now the tall Ragman looked upon this child with pity, and he drew a lovely yellow bonnet from his cart.

"Give me your rag," he said, tracing his own line on her cheek, "and I'll give you mine."

The child could only gaze at him while he loosened the bandage, removed it, and tied it to his own head. The bonnet he set on hers. And I gasped at what I saw: for with the bandage went the wound! Against his brow it ran a darker, more substantial blood—his own!

"Rags! Rags! I take old rags!" cried the sobbing, bleeding, strong, intelligent Ragman.

The sun hurt both the sky, now, and my eyes; the Ragman seemed more and more to hurry.

"Are you going to work?" he asked a man who leaned against a telephone pole. The man shook his head.

The Ragman pressed him: "Do you have a job?"

"Are you crazy?" sneered the other. He pulled away from the pole, revealing the right sleeve of his jacket—flat, the cuff stuffed into the pocket. He had no arm.

"So," said the Ragman. "Give me your jacket, and I'll give you mine."

Such quiet authority in his voice!

The one-armed man took off his jacket. So did the Ragman—and I trembled at what I saw: for the Ragman's arm stayed in its sleeve, and when the other put it on he had two good arms, thick as tree limbs; but the Ragman had only one.

"Go to work," he said.

After that he found a drunk, lying unconscious beneath an army blanket, an old man, hunched, wizened, and sick. He took that blanket and wrapped it round himself, but for the drunk he left new clothes.

And now I had to run to keep up with the Ragman. Though he was weeping uncontrollably, and bleeding freely at the forehead, pulling his cart with one arm, stumbling for drunkenness, falling again and again, exhausted, old, old, and sick, yet he went with terrible speed. On spider's legs he skittered through the alleys of the City, this mile and the next, until he came to its limits, and then he rushed beyond.

I wept to see the change in this man. I hurt to see his sorrow. And yet I needed to see where he was going in such haste, perhaps to know what drove him so.

The little old Ragman—he came to a landfill. He came to the garbage pits. And then I wanted to help him in what he did, but I hung back, hiding. He climbed a hill. With tormented labor he cleared a little space on that hill. Then he sighed. He lay down. He pillowed his head on a handkerchief and a jacket. He covered his bones with an army blanket.

And he died.

Oh, how I cried to witness that death! I slumped in a junked car and wailed and mourned as one who has no hope—because I had come to love the Ragman. Every other face had faded in the wonder of this man, and I cherished him; but he died. I sobbed myself to sleep.

I did not know—how could I know?—that I slept through Friday night and Saturday and its night, too.

But then, on Sunday morning, I was wakened by a violence.

Light—pure, hard, demanding light—slammed against my sour face, and I blinked, and I looked, and I saw the last and the first wonder of all. There was the Ragman, folding the blanket most carefully, a scar on his forehead, but alive! And, besides that, healthy! There was no sign of sorrow nor of age, and all the rags that he had gathered shined for cleanliness.

Well, then I lowered my head and, trembling for all that I had seen, I myself walked up to the Ragman. I told him my name with shame, for I was a sorry figure next to him. Then I took off all my clothes in that place, and I said to him with dear yearning in my voice: "Dress me."

He dressed me. My Lord, he put new rags on me, and I am a wonder beside him. The Ragman, the Ragman, the Christ!

—From *Ragman and Other Cries of Faith* by Walter Wangerin, Jr.
(Harper & Row, 1984)

GOD THE HOLY SPIRIT

The presence and power of the Holy Spirit

Overview

Your students may or may not be familiar with the Holy Spirit. A few may recognize his work in their daily lives, but for many the Holy Spirit is a source of confusion. This service is designed to help your students worship God the Holy Spirit, understand his role, and recognize his presence and power in their lives.

Elements of worship

- Interpretive reading
- Opening prayer
- Special music
- What God says about it
- Object lessons
- Praise and worship through singing
- Reflection, meditation, and prayer to the Holy Spirit

Volunteers needed

- Male actor for the opening reading
- Student to lead in prayer

Materials checklist

- ☐ Copy of script for actor: **Pentecost as I Saw It: An Eyewitness Account** (page 51)

- ☐ Costume robe for interpretive reading "Pentecost as I Saw It"

- ☐ Accompaniment track or recording for special music, "Breathe on Me"

- ☐ A work glove, a bucket of sand, and a small trowel or cup

- ☐ Small, lightweight sign with LIFE written on it

- ☐ A helium tank and one deflated balloon (or one large helium-filled balloon, and one deflated balloon). Tie the deflated balloon to the LIFE sign. During your talk you will fill up the balloon with helium and watch it rise up, lifting the sign. If you don't have a helium tank, just have a second LIFE sign tied to an already inflated balloon. Try this in advance to make sure your balloon will lift your sign.

- ☐ Music for group worship:
  First set
  - "Come Let Us Worship and Bow Down"
  - "Search My Heart"
  Second set
  - "Spirit of God"
  - "Spirit of the Living God (Fall afresh on me)"
  Third set
  - "More Love, More Power"
  Fourth set
  - "Shine, Jesus, Shine"

- Soloist or ensemble for special music
- Student to read closing Scripture

✚　　✚　　✚　　✚　　✚　　✚　　✚

Opening reading
(4-5 minutes)

The interpretive reading **Pentecost as I Saw It: An Eyewitness Account** (page 51) is the fictitious account of one who witnessed the Day of Pentecost, when God sent his Holy Spirit (Acts 2). The reading introduces your students to the Holy Spirit and helps prepare them for the theme of the worship service.

Opening prayer
(2 minutes)

After the reading, have a student lead your group in an opening prayer asking God to reveal himself through his Holy Spirit during this service.

special music option

(5 minutes)

"Breathe on Me" is a beautiful song describing one person's desire for the power, refreshment, and inspiration of the Holy Spirit. If appropriate, use the song as an offertory. Have the music begin immediately following the prayer.

What God says about it
(20 minutes)

The person, presence, and power of the Holy Spirit

Next, move right into your teaching time. The instruction in this lesson is designed to introduce students to the person of the Holy Spirit as God, help them see that he lives within them, and challenge them to live by his power and not their own.

Introduction

1. According to some surveys, up to 90 percent of Christian teens have a hard time explaining just who the Holy Spirit is and how he works in their life.
2. There are three "P's" I'd like us to look at today to help us better understand and remember who the Holy Spirit is and how he works in our lives.

His Person

1. Briefly recount the story of Ananias and Sapphira (Acts 5:1-4) which clearly teaches that the Holy Spirit is God ("you have lied to the Holy Spirit...you have lied to God," verses 3-4).

2. The Holy Spirit is God. He has existed forever as God within the Trinity (Genesis 1:2). He goes out from the Father God and Jesus (John 15:26) and should be recognized and worshiped as God (Matthew 28:19).
3. If the Holy Spirit is God, then let's pray to him now.

Most of your students probably have never addressed a prayer to the Holy Spirit, but this will help them expand their understanding and experience of the

Holy Spirit as God.

Ask your students to take a minute to pray to the Holy Spirit on their own. Or you may wish to have several students lead the group in prayers to the Holy Spirit.

His Presence

1. Not only is the Holy Spirit God, he is God inside us!
The Bible tells us in Ephesians 1:13-14 that when we trust Christ as our Savior we receive the Holy Spirit. Therefore, we do not worship a God who is distant and uninvolved in our lives, but one who has chosen to actually live inside us!

2. *[Object lesson: glove]* **An empty glove is void of any power or function, but when a hand is placed inside, it comes alive and does what the person using it wants.** *[Illustrate this with the limp glove and then place your hand inside.]*
In the same way, the Holy Spirit inside us is like the hand of God within our lives; he gives us direction, gives us power to live the life God would have us live, and fills us with emotions that go beyond our normal human experience— such as joy or peace despite seemingly tough circumstances.
If a glove or the fingers of a glove are full of something then you can't put your hand in. *[Fill the glove with sand from your bucket as you speak.]* **In the same way, if you are filling your life up with other things (pride, busyness, rebellion, etc.) then the Holy Spirit can't take control. We need to identify and eliminate the things that keep the Holy Spirit from filling and controlling every area of our lives (1 Corinthians 6:19-20).** *[Pour out the sand and place your hand inside once again.]*

His Power
1. Object lesson: helium balloon

The Holy Spirit is our source of power to live the Christian life. The Holy Spirit that lives within each believer is the same one that has healed the sick, brought revival, caused miracles, and even raised the dead. Yet as believers, we often neglect to tap into the Holy Spirit's power, choosing instead to rely on our own weak efforts to deal with the problems and spiritual challenges of life.
[On a table have your LIFE *sign tied to the deflated balloon.]* **On our own, we are like that balloon: deflated, defeated, largely powerless.** *[After this explanation, fill up the balloon with helium and watch it rise, lifting the sign. If you don't have a helium tank, just have a second* LIFE *sign tied to an already inflated balloon.]*
This helium is odorless, colorless, and invisible. And yet, when released, it has the power to fly. When we release the Holy Spirit to do his work in our life we will experience his supernatural power to live.

2. Ephesians 3:16 also reminds us that it is the Holy Spirit who strengthens us with power. The Greek word for power is *dunamis,* **from which we get our word for dynamite. We have the same Spirit that raised Christ from the dead! That's power!**

3. One test for the evidence of the Holy Spirit's power working in our lives is found in the Fruit of the Spirit. *[Read Galatians 5:22-23 to your students and ask them to reflect for a moment on which fruits are evident within their lives. Then ask* *them to consider which ones are missing.]*

4. Finally, the Holy Spirit gives special talents/interests to each believer, called spiritual gifts, for the building up of the body of Christ. *[You may want to identify several spiritual gifts and have your students consider which one(s) they've received. But more than just receiving, are they using them? The gifts are listed in 1 Corinthians 12:7-11, Romans 12:4-8, and Ephesians 4:11-12.]*

Worship through music, prayer, and meditation
(15-20 minutes)

Turn the lights down low and ask your students to get on their knees in preparation for worship. Tell the students to sing and pray *to God the Holy Spirit* at his prompting while they are kneeling. Inform them that the worship will be broken up into several segments where they will be encouraged to confess sin, give thanks, and desire the Holy Spirit's working in their lives.

Conviction of the Holy Spirit
As students are kneeling and in an attitude of prayer, open with the following two songs. As the students sing, have them pray that the Holy Spirit would reveal to them areas in their lives where they need to grow. Explain to them that the Holy Spirit will probably bring thoughts, words, or situations to their minds. The students shouldn't just assume that they have thought these suggestions up themselves, but should trust that it may be the Holy Spirit speaking to them.

Or more simply, have them examine their lives in light of the Fruit of the Spirit. Have them confess and get things right with God during this time.

Song suggestions:
• "Come Let Us Worship and Bow Down"
• "Search My Heart"

Thanking the Holy Spirit for his work in our lives
The students can return to their seats if they like. Ask your students to think of ways the Holy Spirit has been at work in their lives and in your group. After singing the songs below, encourage them to share spontaneous praises of thanksgiving aloud from where they're seated (or kneeling). They can begin each sentence prayer with the words, "Holy Spirit, I thank you for —" (in other words, a "popcorn"-type prayer).

Song suggestions:
• "Spirit of God"
• "Spirit of the Living God (Fall afresh on me)"

Inviting the Holy Spirit to take control
Finally, ask students to invite the Holy Spirit to take control over their lives; asking him to fill them, guide them, and give them power to live a holy life and to do God's work.

Song suggestion: "More Love, More Power."

Closing benediction and song
Have students stand and take the hand of the person next to them in the "unity and fellowship of the Holy Spirit." Have the student you chose earlier read the closing blessing from Ephesians 3:20-21.

Close your service in celebration with the song "Shine, Jesus, Shine."

An eyewitness account
Pentecost as I Saw It

Hey. My name's Samuel. I'm a Jew from the tribe of Benjamin, although I've lived most of my life in Egypt. I want to tell you about an amazing event. I'm still not quite sure what really happened that day, but I know it changed my life.

I was in Jerusalem for the Feast of Weeks—that's the Jewish celebration for the wheat harvest, which our Greek overlords call Pentecost. Thousands of Jews from every nation were gathered there. It was exciting, but a little tough for me since I speak only Egyptian. Getting a room—even ordering a meal—was tough.

One morning I walked out into the marketplace to buy some breakfast when I saw a crowd gathering around a group of about a dozen men. I could see they were Galileans—trust me, it isn't hard to spot a Galilean. What got my attention wasn't the number of people—though there were a lot of them—but the noise. It was gibberish—all those Galileans were shouting nonsense. Still drunk from partying the night before, I assumed. Then I got closer—and I heard not gibberish, but actual languages.

And among the bits and pieces of Hebrew and Greek and Latin I recognized, I heard it *my* tongue—Egyptian! One of these people was speaking Egyptian! But a *Galilean*—an uneducated tradesman—speaking my language? How was it possible? I looked around and realized that everyone there, regardless of their race or nation, was hearing these men in their own languages. Even more amazing, though, were the words these men were speaking.

One of them—the one they called Peter—stood up and addressed the entire crowd. They weren't drunk, he said, but filled with—get this—the power of the Holy Spirit. He quoted our prophet, Joel, who prophesied that one day the Lord God would pour out his Holy Spirit on all people and that everyone who called on the name of the Lord would be saved.

Then Peter made the audacious claim that Jesus of Nazareth—a small-town prophet I heard was crucified here a few weeks ago for treason or blasphemy or something—was in fact our promised Messiah. He had been put to death and buried—yet God miraculously raised him from the dead. Sounds ridiculous, I know—but this Peter and a bunch of others apparently saw him alive, walking and talking and eating.

Something about this speech cut into me so deeply, I knew it was the truth. As improbable as it sounded, something inside me knew that what he was saying was right.

Next thing I knew I shouted at the speaker, "So what should we do, then?"

"Repent and be baptized," Peter yelled back over the crowd, "and you will be forgiven of your sins and receive the gift of the Holy Spirit!"

Well, that's about it. Thousands of us believed that day. True to his word, God filled me with his Holy Spirit. I can't tell you the joy I feel actually having God living in me!

CANDLELIGHT COMMUNION

Remembering Christ's death

Overview

This service will provide a meaningful worship experience for your students as they take the Lord's Supper and remember Christ's sacrifice for their sins. Students will participate "in community" as they share the Lord's Supper with one another. The service is highlighted by a choral reading that helps students understand the meaning of communion. The candlelighting at the end of this service beautifully symbolizes that Christ is in us.

Elements of worship

The following elements build upon one another to create an atmosphere of worship, reflection, and renewal as your group shares communion together.
• Open under discipline of silence
• Choral reading
• Opening prayer
• What God says about it
• Scripture reading
• Prayer and meditation time for putting things right with God and with other youth group members
• Worship through singing
• Communion
• Candlelighting
• Special music

Volunteers needed

• Three readers for the choral reading **Remember** (page 56)
• Student to open in prayer
• Soloist for special music

Room preparation

Since the focus of this service is communion, place the table with the elements on it at the front of your room. Have three large candles lit behind the elements representing the Trinity. In addition to the communion elements, the table should also have a supply of small unlit household candles

Materials checklist

☐ Three large decorative candles to light the communion table

☐ Overhead transparency, slide, sign—or slip of paper for each chair—that says—
   BE STILL AND KNOW
   THAT I AM GOD.
   PSALM 46:10

☐ Instrumental praise tape (optional)

☐ Copies of the choral reading **Remember** (page 57) for the three readers

☐ Music for group worship:
   • "Abba Father" (The Family Song)
   • "Search My Heart"
   • "Humble Thyself"
   • "It's Your Blood"
   • "White as Snow"
   • "All I Need Is You"

☐ Communion elements

☐ Candles for everyone (drip shields recommended)

☐ Accompaniment tape or recording for special music, "How Beautiful"

(preferably with drip shields), one for each student. The room should be dark or dimly lit, save for the three candles. Some additional lighting may be needed for those doing the choral reading and the instructional time.

Seating will vary depending on your room and the size of your group. If using chairs, arrange them in a semi-circle with plenty of room for students to get up and move around. If your group is smaller you may wish to have them seated in a circle on the floor for a more intimate setting.

Opening
(5 minutes)

Put your students under a "discipline of silence" as they enter your room.

The overhead transparency of Psalm 46:10 (or slide, or slips of paper with that verse written on them) should be in place.

Let the message speak for itself as your students take the time of silence to quiet themselves before the Lord and experience his presence.

option

If you don't think your students can handle complete silence, you can play instrumental praise music quietly in the background.

Choral reading
(3 minutes)

Remember (page 57) focuses students on the communion elements and how important it is to Christ that we remember his death on the cross.

Opening prayer
(1-2 minutes)

Following the choral reading, have a student stand at her seat and lead in prayer. The prayer should focus on Christ's death on the cross, mentioning his sacrifice which paid for our sins, his unconditional love, forgiveness, and the promise of salvation.

What God says about it
(10-15 minutes)

Through the Word, help students understand that unity with one another in the body of Christ is crucial as they remember and celebrate Christ's death on the cross for their sins. The following is a brief outline to help students prepare for the Lord's Supper.

• ***Communion is taken "in-community."*** Read Acts 2:42 and remind students that the early church also used to take communion together as a way to remember the death of Christ on the cross.

• ***Unity and Christian love are essential as we remember the Lord's death.*** Read 1 Corinthians 11:17-22. Basically, the church at Corinth was rebuked by the Apostle Paul for participating in the love feast in an unworthy manner. They came together for a meal and celebrated the Lord's Supper, but some were selfish with their food and did not share with others. They were not unified.

Ask your students if they are unified with one another. Tell them that Matthew 5:23-24 suggests that if they are in conflict with others in the group, they should make things right *before* worshiping God through communion. Inform students that they will have an opportunity later in the service to go to others in the group if they need to ask forgiveness or forgive someone.

• *Unifying ourselves in Christian love then frees us to focus on the true meaning of the Lord's Supper: to remember Christ's death on the Cross for our sins.* Read 1 Corinthians 11:23-28 and remind your students of the importance and significance of the bread and the wine symbolizing the brutalized body and shed blood of Christ—what he went through for their sins.

Alert your students to the importance of *examining* themselves in light of their relationships with others and with the Lord. (The Greek word behind the English word *examine* has to do with testing metals.) The Bible teaches that they should get things right before taking communion so as not to partake in an unworthy manner.

Communion
(15-20 minutes)

During the communion time, praise, worship, and special music will be woven together to provide a worshipful and prayerful atmosphere as your students prepare themselves to take the Lord's Supper.

Time of reflection and self-examination

Make the transition from your instruction time by moving into praise and worship (see music for group worship). Encourage your students to go to those in the group they may need to speak with before taking communion. Let students go quietly to one another as the rest of the group participates in worship and personal reflection.

Communion

As students are individually ready, have them get out of their seats to take communion. Have them serve themselves or be served as your tradition dictates. Better yet: to freshen the impact, offer the elements in a different form than your students might normally get at your church—fresh bread instead of wafers, juice or wine in a goblet instead of individual-servings communion cups, etc.

Candles

After students have taken communion, have them take and light candles and return to their seats with them. The students will continue in worship until all of the students have gone forward. The room will gradually become filled with light.

Closing song
(5 minutes)

As the last of your students are taking communion, have a student or leader sing the song, "How Beautiful," or play the recording. A popular wedding song, the words actually speak of the body of Christ and the sacrifice he made for the church.

Benediction/closing blessing

With your room filled with candlelight, end the service by blessing your students with these words from 1 Peter 2:9:

But you are a chosen people, a royal priesthood, a holy nation, a people

belonging to God, that you may declare the praises of him who called you out of darkness into his wonderful light.

Remember
A Choral Reading For Three Readers

Reader 1: Now, while I am with them, their faith is so strong, their hearts so sure. They think they will always feel this way. But when I'm gone and times get tough, how will they remember?

Readers 2 & 3: *(softly)* Remember, Remember

Reader 1: They need a symbol

Reader 2: An image

Reader 3: A special ceremony

Reader 1: To help them remember

Readers 2 & 3: *(building slightly)* Remember, Remember

Reader 2: Gold, why not gold? For you are as precious as gold.

Reader 1: No, gold makes you selfish and worldly and proud.

Reader 3: Stone, why not stone? For you are our rock.

Reader 1: No, a stone has no life and can bring too much harm.

Reader 2: Water then, water. You are living water.

Reader 1: No. Water brings life, true. But only my death brings eternal life. More than my life you must remember my death.

Readers 2 & 3: *(still building, gradually)* Remember, Remember

Reader 1: My death, they can never forget my death. Bread and wine, my body and blood.

Reader 2: Bread

Reader 3: His body, crushed, beaten, tortured

Reader 1: Just like this bread is broken, my body will be broken, too. When you come together I want you to eat bread like this and remember me.

Reader 2:	Wine
Reader 3:	His blood. Flowing from every wound.
Reader 1:	Take a drink of this wine and pass it around. My blood is going to be poured out just like you pour this wine. When you come together, drink some wine and remember me.
Reader 2:	As we take these elements into our bodies, we will remember your body.
Reader 3:	Bread
Reader 1:	*(quietly)* Remember
Reader 2:	Wine
Readers 1 & 3:	*(with more intensity)* Remember
Reader 1:	I did it all for you. Do this for me, and remember.
All:	*(intensely)* Remember
Readers 2 & 3:	Yes Lord, we will remember. We will remember you.

—END—

A SIGN, A REALITY

A baptismal service

Overview

Throughout the history of the church, Christians of all traditions have practiced baptism in response to Christ's command that his followers "make disciples of all the nations, baptizing them in the name of the Father and of the Son and of the Holy Spirit" (Matthew 28:19).

For many students, their baptism is a beautiful and important symbol of their spiritual growth and commitment to Christ. For some, however, baptism is just an obligation done to please parents or church leaders. Others are just confused about it: sprinkle, pour, or immerse? What if I was baptized as a baby? What if I wasn't? What if I don't feel ready?

The goal of this service is not necessarily to answer every concern about baptism, but to provide a framework for creating a memorable and meaningful worship experience centered on a celebration of baptism—a service that will build understanding, appreciation, and community.

Materials checklist

List may vary depending upon the worship elements selected.

- ☐ Music for group worship:
  - "Lord, I Lift Your Name on High"
  - "White as Snow"
  - "It's Your Blood"
  - "Nothing but the Blood of Jesus"
  - "As the East Is from the West"

- ☐ Instrumental praise tape

- ☐ Prepared student art. Have several of your more artistic students prepare a piece of "worship art" to share at the service. Paintings, drawings, banners, sculptures, even a music composition, poem, or performance would be appropriate to share as a worship response to God.

- ☐ Copies for all students of **Buried with Him through Baptism**, a responsive reading based on Matthew 28:19, Romans 6:3-5, and Acts 22:16 (page 64).

- ☐ Bowl of water and several dry towels

- ☐ Baptism necessities (robes, towels, etc.)

- ☐ Ask students who are being baptized to think about what they'd like to share. This beautiful time of commitment will be made even more meaningful as students being baptized share their own testimonies of what God has done in their lives, bringing them to the point of baptism.

- ☐ Accompaniment track or recording for special music, "I Surrender All" (not the traditional; see index)

- ☐ Certificates of baptism signed by youth group members. Your church may or may not give baptismal certificates. In place of, or in addition to a church certificate, consider creating your own certificates and have them signed by everyone in the youth group. By signing the certificates, your group is pledging their support and encouragement to those being baptized to help them live for the Lord as well as welcoming them into the family of believers.

Because of differing church baptism traditions, questions of who, where, what, when, and how may be determined by your church. Therefore, you may have to filter the ideas presented in this service. These suggestions should spark your own creativity and help you customize the perfect baptism service for your group.

Capitalizing on the symbolic nature of baptism, this service uses several other symbolic representations of worship including art and a ceremonial cleansing to remind all of the participants of their own renewal in Christ.

Elements of worship
- Opening prayer
- Songs of response
- Unique presentation of art as worship
- Responsive reading to bring understanding of baptism
- Devotional from God's Word
- Object lesson—a moving symbolic cleansing with water
- Baptisms
- Testimonies from those getting baptized
- Special music
- Closing prayer

Volunteers needed
- Family member of someone being baptized to open in prayer
- Students to prepare "worship art"
- Soloist or ensemble for special music

Location
This service is designed with a church facility and traditional baptistry in mind. If your church prefers to do baptisms during regular service times, perhaps you can coordinate this event as a special youth-led service for your church.

However to enhance this already meaningful experience, consider an alternate setting such as a local river, lake, beach, or even a family or camp pool (sunsets and sunrises are especially beautiful). Most of the elements in this service may be easily adapted for an outside setting.

Be sure to invite the parents of the students being baptized, for a young person's baptism is usually a very important event to the family.

Opening prayer
(2 minutes)

Invite a family member of one of the students being baptized to offer the opening prayer. The prayer should focus on thanking Christ for his death on the cross and how his sacrifice cleanses us from our sins. Thank the Lord for each person being baptized as they commit to living their lives for the Lord.

Transition
(1 minute)

Christian baptism is a worship experience for everyone, not just those being baptized. Encourage students to reflect upon their own relationships with God as they sing, pray, and participate in the service.

Songs of response
(5-10 minutes)

Praise the Lord with several songs of response that deal with our salvation and how our sins have been washed away in Christ.

- "Lord, I Lift Your Name on High"
- "White as Snow"
- "It's Your Blood"
- "Nothing but the Blood of Jesus"
- "As the East Is From the West"

Worship art
(5 minutes)

As your worship time draws to a close, continue an instrumental background or praise tape as your "worship art" students come to the front. Just as baptism is a symbol of our relationship with Christ and his sacrifice for us, we as believers can worship God in a number of symbolic, yet very valid ways.

Have the students share their pieces of worship art in turn, describing the art and how it symbolizes or represents their relationships with God.

Responsive reading
(2-3 minutes)

Ask your students to refer to the responsive reading **Buried with Him through Baptism** as they affirm together the importance of Christian baptism through the teachings of Scripture.

option

If a responsive reading is not appropriate for your service or location, or if you desire an additional element at this point in the service, ask one of the parents or adult leaders to share briefly about the time when they were baptized and the significance it has had in their own life.

Devotional from God's Word
(10 minutes)

This brief devotional is meant to provide an understanding of what baptism is all about. It is not intended to answer every issue associated with baptism, nor is it meant to be a doctrinal statement for any one particular viewpoint. If necessary, you may need to adjust what you share in this section to better fit your church's beliefs and practices.

Introduction
Begin by sharing with your students what baptism resembles:

- *Pledge of Allegiance*—symbolizes and represents our citizenship and devotion to our country.
- *High school colors or uniforms*—identify you with your particular classmates and school.
- *Wedding ring*—represents the devotion, commitment, and love one has for his or her spouse.

Like a pledge, team colors, or a wedding ring, baptism symbolizes important truths about our relationship with Jesus. Each one of you can better understand the practice of baptism and respond with an attitude of worship as we unfold two mysteries of the faith.

Mystery 1—Through baptism, we identify ourselves with Christ.

1. Read Romans 6:2-5. Baptism pictures the death, burial, and resurrection of Christ. Going down into the water symbolizes the individual dying to his former self. Coming out of the water symbolizes that the person is now alive in Christ and will defeat spiritual death and live forever with God in heaven.

2. Ring analogy: remind students that there is nothing magical in the water, just like there is nothing magical about a wedding ring. What matters is that the wedding ring represents the love and commitment shared by two people and the act of baptism represents the commitment a person has to Christ.

Mystery 2—Baptism is an outward sign of an inward reality.

1. One of the uses of water is for washing and cleansing. Share with your students that when we become Christians, we become new persons in Christ. By trusting Christ as Savior, our sins are forgiven—washed away (Acts 22:16)—and we receive the gift of the Holy Spirit (1 Corinthians 12:13) and the promise of eternal life (Ephesians 2:8-9, Acts 2:38).

2. Inwardly we are cleansed. Being baptized with water is an outward representation of our inner cleansing.

Transition

Close by sharing with your students that in celebrating the baptisms of fellow group members, we should remember the continual cleansing we receive from Christ as we confess and receive forgiveness (as 1 John 1:9 says: "If we confess our sins, he is faithful and just and will forgive us our sins and purify us from all unrighteousness"). Remembering this should also make us grateful to God and prompt us to worship him.

Object lesson—Cleansing water
(5 minutes)

Invite the whole group to pray silently for those being baptized and to meditate on their own relationships with God. Encourage them to confess their sins to God and receive his cleansing forgiveness.

After the students have had a few moments to meditate, pass around a bowl of water and have them dip a finger or thumb into the bowl. As they dip, have them turn to the persons next to them and make a symbol of the cross on their foreheads with their dampened fingers. As they perform this symbolic "cleansing" with water, have them say the phrase, "The blood of Christ washes away your sins."

If done in an attitude of worship and reverence, this will be a very meaningful experience for your students.

Baptisms
(10-20 minutes depending on number of students)

Your students should be in place and ready for their baptisms. Taking one at a time, have students share their personal testimonies about the difference Christ has made in their lives and their desire to follow him; then perform the baptism.

After students are baptized, have them change back into their clothes and prepare to be prayed for by the entire group to close the service.

Transition
(5 minutes)

Immediately following the baptisms have a student, leader, or ensemble sing "I Surrender All" (not the traditional—see "Special Music" index, page 94) or another appropriate song. The song will help celebrate the baptisms and provide time for the baptized students to change.

Closing prayer
(2-3 minutes)

Close your service by having everyone stand and gather around those just baptized and pray for them. If appropriate, you might want to lay hands on them. Thank God through your prayers for his cleansing and for the salvation we have in Christ. Pray specifically for each individual baptized, that they will continue to live every day of their lives fully for God.

Buried with Him through Baptism

A Responsive Reading Based
on Matthew 28:19, Romans 6:3-5, and Acts 22:16

Leader
Therefore go and make disciples of all nations.

Students
Baptizing them in the name of the Father and of the Son and of the Holy Spirit.

Or do you not know that all of us who were baptized into Christ Jesus were baptized into his death?

We were therefore buried with him through baptism into death in order that, just as Christ was raised from the dead through the glory of the Father, we too may live new lives.

If we have been united with him like this in his death, we will certainly also be united with him in his resurrection. And now what are you waiting for?

Get up, be baptized and wash your sins away, calling on his name.

PRAYER TOUR

Using the A.C.T.S. model of prayer

Overview

Prayer is a powerful aspect of a relationship with God. Imagine the privilege of talking to almighty God—who actually invites us to chat with him. Yet many students struggle with prayer. Some aren't sure just what prayer does. Others want to pray but don't really know how. A few may even think prayer is a waste of time and wonder if God really listens, or even cares.

This very nontraditional worship service will push your students to understand and experience prayer in new and creative ways. Using the familiar A.C.T.S. model of prayer (adoration, confession, thanksgiving, supplication) this service is almost a prayer "tour." But as they go, students will be stretched and motivated to worship God and take their prayer lives to a new level.

Elements of worship

These elements are included to help shape this unique and nontraditional service using the A.C.T.S. model.
- Provocative sketch (optional)
- Humorous and pointed video options
- Reading/story (optional)
- Self-produced video (optional)
- Fresh look at the Lord's Prayer (optional)
- Use of different locations
- What God says about it
- Student-led prayer, sharing, and reading
- Worship through singing
- Special music/prayer of confession
- Personal inventory, reflection, and meditative prayer
- Written prayers of petition
- Object lesson

Materials checklist

Materials may vary depending on the options you choose to include.

- ☐ Two copies of the sketch **If God Should Speak** (page 71). An offstage microphone is helpful.

- ☐ *God Views* video (the relevant segment is summarized on page 66; order from Youth Specialties by calling 800/776-8008). Or create your own video:
  - Interview randomly selected students at school and ask them what prayer is and if they do it.
  - Film a montage of students saying meaningless prayers, or prayers with dubious motivations: "Dear God, save the world...Bless the missionaries...If you just let me pass this test, I'll never cheat again." Or quote a children's prayer poem, like "Now I lay me down to sleep..." Get as creative as possible in making students think about how they really approach prayer in their own lives.

- ☐ Overhead transparency or slide of the Lord's Prayer (optional)

- ☐ Music for group worship:
  - "Great Is the Lord"
  - "How Majestic Is Your Name"
  - "Glorify Thy Name"
  - "Majesty"
  - "Sweet Adoration"

- ☐ Accompaniment track or recording for special music, "Down on My Knees"

- ☐ 3 x 5 cards, white cardstock, and pencils for everyone

- ☐ Toys from the church nursery (no need to remove them—you'll use them *in* the nursery; optional)

Volunteers needed

(depends on which options you include)
• Two actors for sketch
• Soloist for special music
• If you have a large group, you may want an adult leader for each "location" of the service

Room preparation

Ideally, each section of this worship service using the A.C.T.S. prayer model will be held in a different location in and around your church facility. Logistically, it may be helpful to do this service mid-week when more rooms are available at your church facility. However, if locations are limited, the service can also be adapted for use within a single room.

If your group is too large or rooms are too small for everyone to go together, divide your students into four separate groups. Have each group start at one of the four locations listed below, then rotate to the next location in the A.C.T.S. order at 20-minute intervals. You should have an adult leader at each location leading the students through the particular worship elements.

• *Adoration*—Emphasize the greatness of God as Creator and Lord with an outdoor location. A grassy area, a rooftop, or a prayer garden would work well. Seating: whatever is most appropriate (sitting on the grass, benches, etc.).
• *Confession*—Take your students to the church worship center, sanctuary, or chapel to emphasize the serious nature of sin and the importance of getting right with God. Seating: pews, kneelers, or chairs, with dim lighting.
• *Thanksgiving*—Go to the fellowship hall—a place where meals are shared and celebrations are held. Seating: a circle of chairs.
• *Supplication*—Emphasize the child-like faith that should accompany our requests before God by taking your students to the church nursery. Seating: the floor.

The service begins with everyone together in your normal meeting room for the opening sketch explanation of the service.

✚   ✚   ✚   ✚   ✚   ✚   ✚

Opening

(5 minutes) Use one or more of these options to open the service.

sketch

If God Should Speak

This humorous yet pointed sketch (page 71) encourages students to take their prayers more seriously. You may choose to preface the sketch by reminding students about the importance of sincere, specific prayer—and how their lives can change when they learn how to pray.

Maybe Tomorrow

story

Use this story to get your students thinking about their prayer lives (page 73).

1) In *God Views* actor Curt Cloninger portrays the various ways our culture pictures God. One segment offers a look at God as a cosmic butler, who waits hand and foot on all our whims. Play this section to provoke your students to think about their own prayers and how we often treat God—wanting him to serve us, but not really knowing him personally. (Order from Youth Specialties by calling 800/776-8008.)

2) Make your own video! Show your own creation of possible approaches to prayer (good and bad—suggestions given previously).

Lord's Prayer
(2 minutes)

Jesus taught his disciples how to pray through what is commonly known as the "Lord's Prayer" (Matthew 6:9-13).

Transition from your introduction by saying something like,

All of us have probably struggled at one time or another with our prayer lives. So, we're going to spend the remainder of our time learning what prayer is and how to make it real in our lives. Jesus taught his disciples how to pray through what is commonly known as the Lord's Prayer. Let's pray that prayer right now to begin our time together.

Have your students stand. Remind them to consider each word of the prayer rather than repeating it mindlessly.

If your students are unfamiliar with the Lord's Prayer, provide it for them on an overhead transparency or slide.

New Dress for the Lord's Prayer

To give your students a fresh look at the Lord's Prayer (as it appears in Matthew 6:9-13), teach it to them from *The Message*, Eugene H. Peterson's translation of the New Testament (NavPress):

> Our Father in heaven,
> Reveal who you are.
> Set the world right;
> Do what's best—
>   as above, so below.
> Keep us alive with three square meals.
> Keep us forgiven with you and forgiving others.
> Keep us safe from ourselves and the Devil.
> You're in charge!
> You can do anything you want!
> You're ablaze in beauty!
>   Yes. Yes. Yes.

Transition
(5 minutes)

Explain to your students that they will be experiencing four different kinds of prayer as they worship God by using the A.C.T.S. model. Don't go into too much detail and explanation here; simply lead your group to the next location of worship.

Adoration
(20 minutes; do this outside)

1. Instruction
Share with students that *adoration* is a common aspect of prayer found in the Bible. But what exactly is adoration, anyway? Give students several minutes to pair up and discuss what they think adoration is. Suggest that they try to think of a person, place, song, etc., that would be an example of something worthy of adoration—a beautiful place, a celebrity, an athlete, a girlfriend.

Have students share their definitions and examples of adoration briefly with the group. You might ask if anyone thought of a very beautiful place, and have them share what words they would use to describe it.

Have several students read examples of adoration from David (Psalm 100) and Paul (1 Timothy 1:17). Give students a minute of silence to consider who God really is. Encourage them to think of as many adjectives as they can to describe him.

2. Worship
Transition from silence into music. Lead students in a time of adoration by singing praises to God. After several songs, have students share spontaneous prayers of adoration to God. For example, "Lord, you are my Creator and I praise your name...Lord, you are faithful and I thank you that I can put my full trust in you."
    Suggested songs:
• "Great Is the Lord"
• "How Majestic Is Your Name"
• "Glorify Thy Name"
• "Majesty"
• "Sweet Adoration"

3. Application
Remind students that A stands for *adoration* and that they should begin their daily times of prayer giving God adoration and praise for who he is.

Confession
(20 minutes; do this in your worship center or sanctuary)

1. Instruction
Although students may often whisper, "God, forgive my sins," few understand confession or its importance to a believer. Have the students try to come up with their own definitions of confession. Prompt discussion with these questions:

• **Is saying "I'm sorry" to God confession?**
• **Is confessing a sin to God that you know you'll commit again confession?**
• **Does God hold you accountable for sins you forget to confess?**

After letting students discuss for a couple of minutes remind them that a biblical understanding of confession includes—
• A spirit of humility.
• Admitting to God acts of disobedience (things we've done, or even things we *haven't* done but should have) that are not pleasing to him.
• Repentance: changing our minds regarding disobedient actions and trying our best not to repeat them.

David's relationship with God restored through confession (Psalm 32:3-5).

Briefly recount the story of David's adultery with Bathsheba and the subsequent cover-up murder of her husband, Uriah (2 Samuel 11). Explain that David hid his sin of adultery and murder from God and others for nearly nine months. Psalm 32:3-4 reveals the pain David experienced as he held on to the secret of his terrible deeds. Yet he finally confessed to God and received forgiveness.

Ask your students if they have or are presently trying to hide their mistakes and sins from God. Have them reflect on how it has affected their relationship with God. Remind students that when we confess our mistakes and acts of disobedience to God (confession isn't for wimps—it takes courage), the Bible promises us that God will forgive our sins and forget them—like they never happened (1 John 1:9).

2. Special music/prayer of confession

Have someone sing the song "Down on My Knees," or play a recording of it. During the song have students search their hearts for the unconfessed sin in their lives. As the song ends they should slip off alone to confess their sins to God and get things right with him. Suggest that they kneel as they seek God and pray. Remind them of the benefits of confession (forgiveness, burdens lifted, emotional and spiritual healing, ability to move on and grow, etc.). Encourage them to be real with God and not just go through the motions.

3. Application

Before moving to the next location, remind students that c stands for *confession* and that it is a crucial aspect of prayer because it makes us right in God's eyes, and keeps our other prayers from being hindered.

Thanksgiving

(20 minutes; do this in your church's equivalant of a fellowship hall)

1. Instruction

Teach students that *thanksgiving* is showing gratitude or appreciation to God for the many things he does for us and how he works in our lives.

Like the ten lepers (Luke 17:11-19), we often focus more on the gift than the giver, and our "attitude of gratitude" is forgotten. For example, when is the last time you thanked your parents for all they do for you? How about a teacher or a coach that has spent extra time with you? What about a youth leader that has gone out of his or her way to show you kindness or help you in some way?

Give students a 3 x 5 card and have them write down people in their lives they have not thanked for something. After they have finished, ask them to share why thanking others is often forgotten or even difficult.

Share with students that giving God thanks should be a part of their prayer lives because God is worthy of not only our adoration but our thanks as well. The apostle Paul encourages Christians to give their cares and worries over to God in an attitude of gratitude (thanksgiving) in Philippians 4:6. 1 Thessalonians 5:18 encourages Christians to "give thanks in all circumstances, for this is God's will for you in Christ Jesus." Ask students to consider how much of their average prayer time is devoted to thanking to God.

2. Prayer of thanksgiving

Lead your students through a brief time of directed prayer. Spend a minute or two on each of the following areas to help students focus on giving thanks to God.

- **Thank God for your parents.**
- **Think of one thing that you are worried about and give it to God with an attitude of thanksgiving.**
- **Thank God for something you own.**
- **Thank God for a friend.**
- **Thank God for a certain teacher that has made an impact on your life.**
- **Thank God for one of your youth leaders who has been there for you.**
- **Thank God for your gifts and talents.**
- **Thank God for something he has done for you within the past week.**

3. Application

Remind students that T is for *thanksgiving*. Every day we have something for which we can be thankful. Encourage students not to take God's gifts for granted but to take time every day to thank him for all that he has done.

Supplication
(20 minutes; do this in the church nursery)

1. Instruction

Explain to the students that *supplication*—that's the S —is simply *asking* God. It is going to God in prayer to ask him for something either for ourselves or someone else.

God wants us to pray for others (intercessory prayer). Paul prayed for his friend Timothy on a regular basis (2 Timothy 1:3) and the churches where Paul ministered prayed for him (1 Thessalonians 5:25). Ask your students what they pray for when they pray for others (health, jobs, doing well in school, making the basketball team, getting to know God, etc.). Ask your students what percentage of their prayer time is devoted to praying for others. Is it enough? Many students may not ever pray for others.

God wants us to pray for ourselves, too. Jesus encourages us to go to God with our needs and concerns and assures us that God knows what we need and hears our prayers (Matthew 7:7-12). Ask your students to respond to the following questions:

Just because we ask God for something, does that mean we will automatically get it? Why or why not? What if it's an unselfish thing, like praying that we'll do better in school or have more patience with our younger brother?

2. Prayer of supplication

Encourage students to approach God in an attitude of dependence and faith as they ask him for various things. You might wish to give each student a sheet of paper on which to write their prayers and list their requests. Turn the lights down low and give them at least five minutes to pray.

option Ask each student to hold a toy from the nursery as they pray as a personal reminder for them to approach God the Father with the faith and dependence of a child.

Conclusion of the A.C.T.S. service

You may want to gather everyone together to close your service with a song or two or simply dismiss your group after finishing all the sections of the service.

If God Should Speak

by Clyde Lee Herring

Pray-er

Our Father, which art in heav—

God

Yes.

Don't interrupt me. I'm praying.

But you called me.

Called you? I didn't call you. I'm praying. Our Father, which art in heaven, hal—

There, you did it again.

Did what?

Called me. You said, "Our Father, which art in heaven." Well, here I am. What's on your mind?

But I didn't mean anything by it. I was, you know, just saying my prayers for the day. I always say the Lord's prayer. It makes me feel good, you know, kind of like getting a duty done.

All right, then. Go right on ahead with your duty.

Hallowed be thy name. Thy—

Hold it! What do you mean by that?

By what?

By "Hallowed be thy name"?

It means...it means...good grief, I don't know what it means! How should I know? It's just part of the prayer. By the way, what <u>does</u> it mean?

It means <u>honored,</u> <u>holy,</u> <u>wonderful</u>.

Hey, that makes sense. I never thought what <u>hallowed</u> meant before. So, uh, thanks. Anyway...Thy kingdom come, they will be done, on earth as it is in heaven. Give us—

Do you really mean that?

Sure. Why wouldn't I?

What are you doing about it?

Doing? Nothing, I guess. I just think it would be kind of neat if you got control of everything down here like you have up there.

Have I got control of you?

I go to church...

That's not what I asked you. What about that habit of telling only half the truth—it's the same as lying, you know. And your temper. That's really becoming a problem. Then there's the way you spend your money—all on yourself. And even <u>you</u> suspect that you've been feeding your imagination inappropriately—you know, the videos you've been watching with—

Okay, already! So stop picking on me! I'm just as good as some of the rest of those people—those <u>phonies</u>—at church.

Excuuuse me! I thought you were praying for my will to be done. If you want my will, it starts with my will for the one praying for it. In this case, <u>you</u>.

Okay. I guess I <u>do</u> have some problems. In fact, I could probably name some others.

So could I.

I haven't thought about it much till now, but I really would like to cut out some of those things. I'd like to be—well, you know, free.

Good. Now we're getting somewhere. We'll work together, you and I. Some victories can truly be won. I'm proud of you!

Look, Lord, I really need to finish up here. This is taking a lot longer than it usually does. Okay, where was I...Give us this day our daily bread—

You'd better cut down on some of that bread. You're overweight as it is.

Just a minute. What is this, Criticize Me Day? Here I was, dong my spiritual duty, and all of a sudden, <u>you</u> break in and remind me of all my problems and shortcomings.

Praying is a dangerous thing. You could wind up changed, you know. That's what I'm trying to get across to you. You called me, and here I am. It's too late to stop now. Keep on praying. I'm interested in the next part of your prayer. (pause) **Well, are you or aren't you going to finish?**

I'm afraid to.

Afraid? Afraid of what?

I know what you'll say next.

Try me and see.

(Pause) Forgive us our trespasses as we forgive those who trespass against us.

What about Dan?

I knew it...see, I just knew you'd bring him up. Why, he's lied about me, cheated me out of some money, and is the biggest hypocrite around. I won't have anything to do with him again, ever.

What about your prayer?

I didn't mean it.

At least you're honest. But it's not fun carrying that load of bitterness around inside you, is it?

No, but I'll feel better as soon as I get even with him.

No you won't. You'll only feel worse. Revenge isn't sweet. Think of how unhappy you are already. But I can change all that.

How?

First forgive Dan. Then the hate and sin will be his problem, not yours. You may lose the money, but you will have settled your heart.

But I can't forgive Dan.

Then how do you expect me to forgive you?

You're always right, aren't you? More than I want to give Dan back what he gave me, I want to be right with you. *(Pause)* Okay, I forgive him. I'll leave it up to you to get him back on the right road. Now that I think about it, he's bound to be miserable, going around doing the things he does. Some way, somehow, show him the right way. Even if you want me to be part of it.

There now! Wonderful! How do you feel?

Well, not as bad as I thought.

You're not finished with your prayer, you know.

Oh yeah, right. And lead us not into temptation, but deliver us from evil.

Yes, yes, I'll do that. Just do your best to avoid situations where you <u>know</u> you'll be tempted.

What do you mean?

Take a hard look at your friendships. Some of your so-called friends are beginning to get to you. Don't be fooled: they advertise that they're having fun, but for you it could be ruin. Either you're going to have to stop hanging out with them, or start being a positive influence among them. Don't use me as an escape hatch.

Escape hatch?

You know what I mean. You've done it lots of times. You get caught in a bad situation. You get into trouble by not listening to me, and then once you do, you come running to me, saying, "Lord, help me out of this mess, and I promise to never do it again." Ah, I can tell you're remembering now.

Yes...and I'm ashamed.

Which, uh, bargain are you remembering?

When Mrs. Thompson—you know, the woman who lives two houses down—drove by the 7-Eleven when me and some friends were smoking out front. I just knew she recognized me. I told you, "Oh God, please don't let her tell my mom what she saw." And I promised to stop hanging around those friends.

Mrs. Thompson didn't tell your mother—but you didn't keep your promise, did you?

Sorry, Lord. Really. Up till now, I thought that if I just prayed the Lord's Prayer every day, then I could do what I like. I didn't expect anything like this to happen.

Go ahead and finish up.

For thine is the kingdom and the power and the glory forever. Amen.

Do you know what would bring me glory? What would make me really happy?

No, but try me. I really want to know. It's more than that, even—I really want to <u>do</u> whatever it is that pleases you.

You just answered my question.

Huh?

What gives me pleasure is people like you loving me enough to want to do my works. And I can tell that's happening now. So now that old sins are exposed and out of the way, there's no telling <u>what</u> we can do together.

Lord, let's see what we can make out of me, okay?

Yeah—let's see!

—END—

—From *Greatest Skits on Earth, Vol. 2: Skits with a Message* (Youth Specialties/Zondervan, 1987). Reprinted and adapted from *If God Talked Out Loud* by Clyde Less Herring. Copyright 1977, Broadman Press. All rights reserved.

Maybe Tomorrow

by S. Rickly Christian

I keep telling myself I need to pray more. But something always comes up. I suppose it's been weeks since I've talked with God. Maybe months. It's hard to remember.

Last night, I planned to go up to my room after dinner, dig my Bible out of my closet, and read a chapter or two. And later, spend some quality time in prayer. But the Bible was tucked under some magazines, which seemed more interesting. You know how it goes sometimes. Then the phone rang. It was just a friend from work who wanted to switch hours with me. But we got to talking about that new girl on the job—the one with the California tan and cover-girl smile. When I hung up and glanced at the clock, I couldn't believe it was already time for my favorite show on TV, a two-hour special.

Before I knew it, the night was shot. I had to take a quick shower and make a sack lunch for school the next day.

It was hard to read my Bible and pray at 11:30 after all that. No energy. I tried, but kept thinking about that new girl and a thousand other things. So I ended up just mumbling a few bless 'ems before drifting off to sleep.

I know I need to pray more. I mean to *really* pray. Other Christians I know say prayer changes things. So it must be important. But time slips away so easily.

Maybe things will be different tomorrow. Yeah, maybe.

Worship Service 10

GOD IS FAITHFUL, PERIOD

Praising God for his unflagging faithfulness

Overview

Today's students come from a generation often characterized as wary, cynical doubters. They don't seem to trust easily whether it's parents, teachers, politicians, or even youth workers. How can we ask them to trust in God who says he is faithful? Do they even understand what faithfulness is? This worship service uses student involvement, a thought-provoking reading, teaching, and a creative personal commitment time. It is designed to help students understand the faithfulness of God and believe that they can trust him to do what he promised—to care and to always be there. When they understand God's faithfulness, it will prompt their worship.

Elements of worship
• Student-led opening prayer, **What If...**
• Scripture reading
• Praise and worship through music
• What God says about it
• Student testimony (one or more)
• Prayer, meditation, and personal object lesson/commitment time
• Special music
• Closing Scripture and prayer

Volunteers needed
• Student to pray the **What If...** prayer
• Two students to read Scripture passages
• Student(s) for testimony(ies) on God's faithfulness
• Soloist or ensemble for special music (optional)

Materials checklist

☐ Copy of **What If...** prayer (page 79)

☐ Music for group worship:
  • "Our God Is Faithful and Able"
  • "The Steadfast Love of the Lord"
  • "I Walk by Faith"
  • "You Are My Hiding Place"
  • "Give Thanks"
  • "You Have Been Good"
  • "You Are So Faithful"

☐ A mock wedding ring for each student (available at any party- or wedding-supply store or craft shop. Optional: tie to each ring a thin satin ribbon, which could be used later as a Bible bookmark)

☐ Accompaniment track or recording for special music, "Fear Not, My Child"

• Student for closing Scripture and prayer

Student-led opening prayer
(2-3 minutes)

Open your time with a prayer of invocation that will get your students' attention. Have a student pray the **What If...** prayer (page 79), or write a similar prayer that forces students to confront both the good and bad of life in the light of God's faithfulness.

Scriptural response
(2 minutes)

What exactly does *faithfulness* mean? Ask the students to respond. Does it mean having someone do what we want them to do? Is it just having someone there for us (whatever we think that means)? Or does faithfulness mean being absolutely true to one's pure character—in God's case, being exactly who he says he is, and doing exactly what he says he'll do?

Have some students read about God's faithfulness from the Bible:
• Lamentations 3:22-23
• Romans 8:28, 38-39

Praise and worship
(15 minutes)

Choose songs dealing with the theme of God's faithfulness. Songs about trust and thanksgiving would also be good. Here are some suggestions:
• "Our God Is Faithful and Able"
• "The Steadfast Love of the Lord"
• "I Walk by Faith"
• "You Are My Hiding Place"
• "Give Thanks"
• "You Have Been Good"
• "You Are So Faithful"

What God says about it: no matter what, he is faithful
(15-20 minutes)

This lesson demonstrates to the students that regardless of the circumstances in their lives, God is faithful to himself and his promises. And because of his goodness, they can trust him. The instruction time is complemented by a student testimony.

Instruction: If God is so faithful, why is my life so miserable? *(5-8 minutes)*
Although your students have just finished praising God for his faithfulness, it's time to shake them up as you raise the question of God's seeming *unfaithfulness* amidst the struggles of life. To begin, ask your students if they have ever felt that God has been absent from their lives during times when they have needed him most.

An awful lot of people don't feel that God is faithful at all. As a matter of fact, many teenagers, if they feel anything for God, feel contempt because all

they see around them is pain and problems.

Trent Reznor of Nine Inch Nails wrote in the song "Heresy":

> His perfect kingdom of killing, suffering and pain
> Demands devotion, atrocities done in his name.
> Your God is dead and no one cares.

Reznor also said (in *USA Today*), "I'm not proud to say I hate myself and I don't like what I am."

It's no wonder youths are losing hope. Listen to these statistics of what happens to teens *every day* in the U.S.:
• More than 2,500 children witness the divorce or separation of their parents.
• About ninety are taken from parents' custody and committed to foster homes.
• About a thousand unwed teenage girls become mothers.
• Thirteen 15-to-24-year-olds commit suicide; sixteen are murdered.
• Some 500 adolescents begin using drugs and 1,000 begin drinking.
• At least 3,610 teenagers are assaulted, 630 are robbed, and 80 are raped.
• More than 100,000 high school students will bring guns to school.
• At least 2,200 will drop out of high school.

About this generation a professor at University of California, Berkeley, said this: "What we're seeing is the complete destruction of the social environment for these kids. Economic opportunity, stable relationships, housing, safety at school, hope for the future; Everything that makes up living has kind of disappeared for them." (From *13th Gen: Abort, Retry, Ignore, Fail?* by Neil Howe and Bill Strauss)

In light of all this, is it any wonder that we might doubt God's faithfulness?

We can't even begin to understand the mysteries of the mind of God or totally understand why he has allowed the pain in our world, and yet I have heard it said that everything in our lives is designed to drive us to the Cross. C.S. Lewis wrote that God whispers in our pleasure, but shouts in our pain. By allowing us to live in an imperfect world, God apparently allows the greater good, and therefore is the most faithful he can be, whether it makes sense to us or not.

Review 2 Corinthians 12:7-10. Talk about Paul's remarkable response to his state of suffering and his regard for the faithfulness of God in his life.

Student Testimony
(2-5 minutes)

Have a student share an experience of hardship in his or her life, and yet was able to see God's faithfulness at work.

Instruction: God is faithful. He is as good as his Word! (5-7 minutes)

1. To believe that God is faithful is an exercise in faith itself. Hebrews 11:1 says that "faith is being sure of what we hope for and certain of what we do not see," and yet the rest of the chapter goes on to detail more than a dozen accounts of people who put their trust in the faithfulness of God and saw miraculous results. An analogy could be flying in an airplane. You put your trust in an airline and the pilot each time you fly. *[If you can, personalize the analogy to fit your own experience.]*

We have the witness of hundreds of people in the Bible who can testify to the faithfulness of God. On top of that, you have the testimony of millions of

Christians, just like *[name the student who gave the testimony earlier in the service]*, **who will say the same. But most importantly, you have God's own words about himself. Here are just a few of the reasons we can praise God for his faithfulness:**
- **God does not change: he is reliable. His years will never end (Psalm 102:25-27).**
- **God's love will never fail us (Romans 8:39).**
- **God will not allow us to be tempted beyond what we can bear, but is faithful to give a way out (1 Corinthians 10:13).**
- **If we confess our sins he promises to forgive us (1 John 1:9).**
- **God has a future and a hope planned for us (Jeremiah 29:11).**

Don't you want to trust someone like that? Don't you long to rest in the care of a God who makes those kind of promises? The world looks dark sometimes, but we need to believe that the loving God who created us has not abandoned us. He has a perspective and a plan far beyond what we can understand. I've come to trust and believe in the faithfulness of God, not because of how it fits into what I want, but because of *who* God is.

Prayer meditation/object lesson
(5-10 minutes)

Close the service by having your students take time to thank God on their own for his faithfulness to them. As they are praying, pass a tray holding mock wedding rings (perhaps tied with a satin ribbon) and ask them each to take one.

A wedding ring is a universal symbol of faithfulness. A man and woman pledge undying commitment to each other regardless of the circumstances. We know that in this day those vows are often broken, but God has made a pledge of faithfulness to us that he will never break. He sealed his vow with Jesus. Have them take a ring and keep it as a reminder of God's constant faithfulness to them. (If the ring is on ribbon, have them keep it as a Bible bookmark; if not, have them wear it the rest of the day to remember God's faithfulness.)

special music option As students are praying and receiving their rings, have someone sing "Fear Not, My Child" or lead a praise song. Have students join in the singing if appropriate.

Before the song, tell the students this: if, when they take their ring, they feel they've been struggling with God's faithfulness—or their unfaithfulness to God—and would like prayer, they can meet right then, privately, with an adult or student leader for prayer. **option**

Closing Scripture and prayer
(2 minutes)

Invite students to stand. Ask a students read Proverbs 3:5-6 and close in prayer.

what if...?

Dear Lord,

What if someone close to me is seriously hurt today?
What if I win a million dollars in a lottery?
What if my boyfriend cheats on me?
What if I get that car I've always wanted?
What if I *never* get that car I've always wanted?
What if my friend overdoses on drugs?
What if my team wins the state championship?
What if my parents split up?
What if I get into the college I really want?
What if I find out I have an incurable disease?
What if I end up in the Army and get sent to a war zone?
What if I become a missionary?
What if I'm tempted in a big way and give in and sin?

Whatever happens, Lord, I will trust in you—
Because you are faithful, and that will never change.

Thank you, Lord, for your faithfulness.
Amen.

PREPOSTEROUS PEACE

Gratitude to God for his peace

Overview

In our world filled with tragedy and conflict, peace often seems like an unknowable thing. And yet, God can grant peace despite the difficult circumstances of our lives. In this service students will explore the peace of God, come to a deeper understanding of how to have God's peace in their lives, and then have the opportunity for a worship response to God for his peace.

Elements of worship

• **Stress Test**, to help students recognize their need for God's peace
• Student testimony
• Meditation—"Lectio Divina"
• What God says about it
• Written student reflection
• Directed prayer
• Worship through music/Scripture reading
• Special music
• Object lesson

Volunteers needed

• Student to give testimony about stress
• Several students to read passages of Scripture during group worship

Materials checklist

☐ Copies of the **Stress Test** (page 85)

☐ Pencils

☐ 3 x 5 card for each student

☐ Music for group worship:
  • "My Peace"
  • "Peace Give I to Thee"
  • "All That I Need (My Only Hope)"
  • "Search My Heart"
  • "Cares Chorus"

☐ Accompaniment track or recording for special music: "Sometimes He Calms the Storm," "The Peace That Passes Understanding," or a similarly appropriate selection

☐ Barbecue or other receptacle for a small ground fire for use at the end of the service

• Soloist or ensemble for special music

✛ ✛ ✛ ✛ ✛ ✛ ✛

Introduction—The Stress Test
(10 minutes)

There is no denying that students today are busy and stressed out. Their daily organizers are packed with appointments, work schedules, practices, homework, and demands from parents. While their lives are chaotic, they may not realize that God can provide relief from their inner turmoil. This introductory exercise will let the students have a little fun as they come to clearly see their need for God's peace.

Although the noise of our modern world is cause for stress, we can be victims of stress even sitting alone in a peaceful place. After all, lack of peace has much more to do with inner turmoil than outer turmoil.

Provide each student with a copy of the **Stress Test** (page 85). After students take and score the test, you may want them to share their results with the person next to them or with the group.

Scripture/testimony
(5 minutes)

At this point a student (one you've prepped ahead of time) gives a brief testimony of an episode in her life when she was really stressed out over something—and kept things in her own hands instead of giving the stress to God. When she's done relating her experience, she reads Philippians 4:6-7 to the group, then closes by pondering aloud what she wished she would've done instead.

Meditation—"Lectio Divina"
(10 minutes)

"Lectio Divina" is a traditional method of small-group meditation during which participants strive to hear God's voice through Scripture. Read Matthew 8:24-27 (Jesus calms the storm) three times to your students. Don't bother introducing or explaining the passage; just let it speak for itself. Have your students close their eyes and meditate upon it. Tell them to see, hear, feel, taste, and smell the verses. Ask them to picture themselves in the passage—who or where are they? Pause between each reading and, by the third time, the object is for students to actually hear God speaking to them through the passage.

After the meditation, ask a few questions to help students evaluate their experience:

• **Who were you in the passage?**
• **What is your storm?**
• **Did you realize that Jesus was in the boat?**
• **Are you having trouble trusting Jesus to calm your storm?**

82

What God says about it
(10-15 minutes)

This section encourages your students to give their concerns, worries, and difficulties to God so they can receive and experience his peace in their lives. It also prompts the students to worship God for his faithfulness as they realize that he cares for them during times of stress.

Reread Philippians 4:6-7. Share with your students that it contains two important principles to remember for experiencing God's peace.

1) Don't be anxious.

First, we are commanded not to be anxious, or overly stressed-out, about anything. This doesn't mean that we shouldn't be concerned about the circumstances, relationships, and situations that affect our lives, but that we should be aware of the consequences we could suffer when we try to handle them without God's help. Remember, we can trust God. he is always faithful to his promises to provide for us, strengthen us, lift us up, and keep our best interests at heart.

Explore this maxim: "Trust strengthens, worry weakens."

Identify—Ask your students to write down on a card a problem, situation, or concern they're facing right now. After they have written it down, ask them to close their eyes and ask themselves how they have been dealing with it (worry, turning to friends, ignoring the problems, etc.). Have them hold their cards.

2) Talk to God about your troubles.

Second, God invites us to go to him in prayer with an attitude of thanksgiving with our requests and concerns. Why are we thankful? Both for his help in the past and for new opportunities to grow, knowing that trials will strengthen our faith and character (James 1:2-3).

• Share and expound on this statement of truth: "Prayer increases faith, lack of prayer increases self."

Pray—Lead the students in a time of directed prayer about the issues on their cards.

• Thank God for who he is. Acknowledge his character qualities and the fact that he is there to help you.
• Thank God for his faithfulness in the past. Be specific.
• Give your situation over to God. Don't tell God what you want him to do. Just give it to him and ask for his will to be done. Ask God to help you release the situation into his hands.

3) Result: Peace!

Granted, it's simplistic to say that following these steps will magically take your students out of their problems and into contented peace. Yet as students begin to follow what God says in Philippians 4, his peace can and *will* come.

Evaluate the theology of the bumper sticker that says NO GOD, NO PEACE—KNOW GOD, KNOW PEACE.

Worship
(10-15 minutes)

Intersperse selected Scripture readings throughout your time of worship. These passages, read by students, are meant to provide encouragement.
• Jeremiah 29:11
• 1 Peter 5:6-7
• Matthew 11:28-30
• Romans 8:28, 37-39
• Psalm 37:3-6
• Psalm 71:5
• Psalm 23
• Colossians 3:15

Suggested song list:
• "My Peace"
• "Peace Give I to Thee"
• "All That I Need (My Only Hope)"
• "Search My Heart"
• "Cares Chorus"

special music option (5 minutes)
Have a soloist or youth ensemble prepare one of these or another appropriate song to continue your time of worship:
• "Sometimes He Calms the Storm"
• "The Peace That Passes Understanding"

Receiving God's peace
(5-10 minutes)

Ask the students to pray one last time over their "concern" cards and, by faith, receive God's peace. Thank him in advance for his faithfulness and provision. Give them a time of silence in which to pray and receive God's peace. As they feel ready, have them individually get up and leave the room. Outside the door, have a small barbecue or ground fire burning. Ask the students to drop their cards into the fire; symbolically giving that problem over to God. Just as it's impossible to retrieve a burned card from a fire, remind them that they need to genuinely and continually give over their problems to God and not take them back to worry over again.

Stress Test

Stress Points

Check those events that you've experienced within the past 12 months. Then total your score.

Stress Points	Event
100	☐ Death of a parent
73	☐ Divorce of parents
70	☐ Death of an immediate family member
65	☐ Sexual abuse or rape
60	☐ Marital separation by parents
59	☐ Jail/correctional institute term
59	☐ Pregnancy out of wedlock (female: abortion, adoption, or keep the baby?)
53	☐ Pregnancy out of wedlock (male)
44	☐ Personal injury or illness (prolonged or serious)
44	☐ Other health problems
42	☐ Death of a close friend
40	☐ Break-up with long-term boyfriend or girlfriend
39	☐ Addition of a new family member
38	☐ Loss of job by one or both parents
36	☐ Major disappointment
35	☐ Marital reconciliation by parents
35	☐ Arguments with either parent or both parents (significant)
30	☐ Multiple extracurricular responsibilities, (sports, clubs, youth leadership, civic, etc.)
29	☐ First job or new job
29	☐ Trouble with boyfriend's or girlfriend's parents
29	☐ Major achievement
28	☐ Poor grades
28	☐ Pressure to experiment with drugs
28	☐ Pressure to surpass sexual limits
25	☐ Break-up with short-term boyfriend or girlfriend (2 months or less)
25	☐ Change in living conditions/move
24	☐ Revision of personal habits
23	☐ Trouble with teacher/principle/coach
20	☐ Death of a favorite pet

_____

Total

	Scoring
175+	Severely over-stressed
150-174	Serious stress
125-149	High level of pressure
100-124	Average pressure level
0-99	You *need* some pressure in your life.

WHAT CAN I GIVE HIM?

Giving our gifts to God

Overview

Sometimes students may see worship as boring and irrelevant to their lives. Perhaps this is because they are seldom asked to participate in ways that are meaningful to them. God has given your students many unique and wonderful gifts and talents with which to glorify him. When was the last time you offered your group an opportunity to use their individual gifts as an expression of worship?

Worship is more than singing praise songs and praying. It is dynamic and can include all of life's experiences (Colossians 3:23-24). Worship *can* be an expression of who we are in Christ as we respond by giving our gifts to God as an offering. The purpose of this service is to broaden your student's understanding that each of them has gifts that can be given as offerings of worship to God.

For example, God has gifted some of your students with athletic abilities, others with musical talents, and still others with artistic gifts. Why can't a football player dedicate every play to God? Or a musician every performance?

The service provided here is really just a sample to give you an idea of how you might structure your own service using the unique gifts, experiences, and abilities of your students. Consider the possibilities below.

Gifts Students Could Offer to God as Expressions of Worship

• Sing (solo or ensemble).
• Dance as an act of worship.
• Play an instrument (solo or ensemble).
• Perform an original musical composition.
• Share a work of art: painting, drawing, sculpture, or something else created with the hands.
• Read an original poem expressing some aspect of the Christian life.
• Perform a dramatic scene or reading.
• Bring food or clothing collected for those in need.
• Give a testimony of how they have used their athletic abilities in response to God.
• Share photographs, videos, or slides taken by students.
• Share prepared food in an act or worship through hospitality.
• Use costumes in the worship service made by someone with a gift for sewing.
• A student who sews or quilts could make a praise banner for your youth room.

Just remember that this isn't a talent show, but a worship service. Explain that God is our audience, and we can worship together with those who are giving their gifts.

Introduction
(2 minutes)

Worship is our response to God and who he is. And although singing and praying are good ways to worship God, they are certainly not the only ways. In fact, we can respond to and glorify God through virtually every gift and area of our lives. God is the audience, but we will also be blessed as we worship together with the students who are here to give their gifts to God today.

Preface each section with a Scripture reading that demonstrates the Biblical precedent for this type of worship. Use one or two students, who aren't already involved in another section of the service, to do the reading.

Read Romans 12:1 or Colossians 3:17 as a final reminder.

Opening "visual" prayer
(2-4 minutes)

Introduce your students to a creative approach to prayer. Have students who are interested in photography put together a short "visual-prayer" slide presentation. Organize the slides in terms of prayer themes: nature (thanking God for his creation), family members, pastors, youth leaders, school campuses, etc. You might wish to include title slides indicating each theme to be prayed for. Have your students pray as they are prompted by the slides.

What God says about it
(10 minutes)

God allows us creativity in the ways we approach worship. Singing, praying, and learning from God's Word are very important aspects of our worship, but certainly not the only ways. God has gifted each of us in unique ways, and we each have special abilities, talents, and gifts to offer to God as personal expressions of worship.

Here are two principles that reveal the importance of giving our gifts to God.

Principle 1—Whatever you do, do it for the Lord! (Colossians 3:23-24)
In context, Paul was trying to encourage Christian slaves to consider their work as being done for the Lord. I think he said this to encourage them and to help them see the bigger picture that everything we do can be offered to God as an expression of our worship to him.

Encourage your students to have the same attitude about the things they do. Whether it's school, sports, clubs, musical or artistic talents, a job, ministry, hobby—whatever they do, wherever they do it, students can do their "things" in honor of God.

For example, Michelangelo painted the ceiling of the Sistine Chapel as a gift to God as he expressed himself through the artistic gifts God had given him.

Or what about a sports figure like Orel Hershiser? He won the world series and the Cy Young award in 1988, and the American League Championship in 1995—and gave the credit to God.

Secondly, Paul says to "do it with all of your heart."

Encourage students to do their best at whatever God has gifted them to do because they are doing it for him! If they serve others by doing yard work or going on a missions trip, they should give their best and worship God through the act. If they dance or sing, encourage students to put their whole heart into it as an act of worship to God.

Principle 2—Be faithful with the gifts God has given you—the parable of the talents *(Matthew 25:14-30).*
Share with your students that like the parable of the talents, God has given each of them "talents" of their own (not financial, but tangible just the same). Have students consider the unique ways God has blessed them. Anything goes. It doesn't have to be great musical, artistic, or athletic abilities. Help them realize that God wants us to faithfully use what he has given us for his glory.

Perhaps some of your students are glory hogs; taking all the credit for themselves. Others might be prideful in the things they can do. Still others lack confidence or are apathetic about giving their gifts to the Lord. Remind students of the opportunities they have to worship God through the use of the gifts he has given them. Such gifts are not to be taken for granted, exploited, or neglected.

Here are examples of some "offerings" students could share.

Singing
(10-15 minutes)
Read Psalm 100:1-2.

Have students lead your group in a time of praise and worship with songs they wrote themselves! You might want to also include some familiar songs if there is a shortage of original material. Singers, guitarists, drummers, etc., can all be a part of a student praise band.

Offering
(5 minutes)
Read Psalm 33:1-5.

Most groups have at least a few students who play instruments. Why not have several of them play a special song for your offertory either as a solo or an ensemble?

Giving works of art as worship
(5 minutes)
Read 2 Chronicles 2:6-7.

Prior to this service, ask several of your students if they will exhibit any examples of fine or practical art they've created—sketches, sculptures, or photos to woodworking or needlework. Make time for any performance art, too. Some kids may want to explain the meaning of their art and how it is an expression of worship for them.

Dancing before the Lord
(5 minutes)

Read Psalm 149:1-3.

Have an individual or ensemble of dancers prepare a dance routine to a Christian song—whether upbeat and celebratory or slower and reverent. Perhaps other students can create the costume(s).

Serving others as an act of worship
(2-5 minutes)

Read Matthew 25:34-40.

Have a student share about an act of kindness or service they did for another person. Have them personalize the Matthew 25 passage as they explain how serving food to a homeless person at a shelter, for example, could actually be doing it unto the Lord.

Athletic testimonies
(5-8 minutes)

Read 1 Peter 2:12.

Ask a pair of athletes in your group—male and female—to explain their dedication to their sports and how they give God the glory and credit for their abilities. The students may show video clips, slides, or simply set up a poster board of photographs or newspaper clippings of their athletic involvement. Have the students each share testimonies of how they give their athletic participation to God and examples of things they have done to take a stand for their faith and to glorify God. After one or two student athletes have shared, invite any other athletes to come forward and receive prayer. Have other students in your group pray for the athletes that they will be strong witnesses for Christ on their respective teams and campuses.

Worship through a song of celebration or praise
(5 minutes)

Read Colossians 3:16.

Wrap up your service with a song of celebration or praise to God sung by an individual or student ensemble.

Closing time of silence and reflection
(5 minutes)

Read Colossians 3:17.

Ask your students to bow their heads for a time of guided spiritual reflection. A student can quietly read an original poem or story dealing with an aspect of the Christian life. If appropriate, the service can be closed with a prayer.

Index to Music and Video Resources Used in This Book

To obtain the music and lyrics of the praise choruses suggested in this book, see the following music resources, available through most Christian bookstores. These eleven books are listed in order of frequency used. (The first book in the list, *Maranatha! Music Praise Chorus Book, Third Edition*, contains most of the choruses suggested in *Worship Services for Youth Groups*.) See the "Songs for Group Singing" index (pages 92-93) for a listing of each song and its corresponding book, and the service(s) in which it is used.

1. *Maranatha! Music Praise Chorus Book, Third Edition* (Word/Maranatha, 1993)

2. *Worship Songs of the Vineyard, Volume One* (Mercy Publishing, distributed by The Benson Co., 1989)

3. *Maranatha! Music Praise Chorus Book, First Edition* (Word/Maranatha, 1983)

4. *Maranatha! Music Songs for the Congregation, Volume One* (Word/Maranatha, 1991)

5. *Hosanna! Music, Songbook 8* (Integrity Music, Inc., 1994)

6. *Hosanna! Music, Songbook 5* (Integrity Music, Inc., 1991)

7. *Songs*, compiled by Yohann Anderson (Songs and Creations, 1982; 415/457-6610)

8. *War Live, Songbook 3* (Seam of Gold, Pub., admin. by Maranatha! Music)

9. *Songs along the Way* (Stream Mountain Music; not available in stores—call 612/490-3050)

10. *The Youth Chorus Book, Volume One*, by Al Denson (The Benson Co., 1990)

11. *Forty Sing-Along Songs for Worship* (The Benson Co., n.d.)

Other Helpful Music Resources
- *Maranatha! Music Praise Chorus Books*, editions 1-3
- *Integrity's Hosanna! Music Praise Worship Songbooks*, volumes 1-9
- *Worship Songs of the Vineyard*, volumes 1-7 (Mercy Publishing)
- *The Youth Chorus Book*, volumes 1-2 (Al Denson/Benson Publishing)
- *The Group Songbook* (Group Publishing)

Songs for Group Singing

These are listed in alphabetical order. The boldface numbers after the titles refer to, first, the service(s) in which the songs appear; then, after the colon, to the songbook in which the song can be found (listed on page 91). So **9:5** after a song title means that the listed song is used in worship service 9, and the song can be found in songbook 5, *Hosanna! Music, Songbook 8* (from page 91). Songs without a second number are traditional.

- "Abba Father" (The Family Song)—**4,7:1**
  Words and music by Steve Hampton
  © 1978, 85 Scripture in Song admin. by Maranatha! Music

- "All I Need Is You"—**1,7:3**
  Words and music by Jim Stipech
  © 1978 Maranatha! Music

- "All That I Need (My Only Hope)"—**11:10**
  Words and music by John Paul
  © 1984, John Paul Trimble Music

- "Almighty"—**4:5**
  words and music by Wayne Watson
  © 1990 Material Music (admin. by Word Music)

- "As the East Is from the West"—**1,8:9**
  Words and music by Bob Stromberg, arr. Rick Carlson
  © 1991 Stream Mountain Music. All rights reserved.

- "Away in a Manger "—**3:1**

- "Awesome God"—**4:1**
  words and music by Rich Mullins
  © 1986 Edward Grant, Inc.

- "Cares Chorus"—**1,11:1**
  Words and music by Kelly Willard
  © 1978, Maranatha! Music

- "Come Let Us Worship and Bow Down"—**6:1**
  words and music by Dave Dougherty
  © 1980 Maranatha! Music

- "Emmanuel" (author unknown)—**3:1**

- "Give Thanks"—**10:1**
  Words and music by Henry Smith
  © 1991 Integrity's Hosanna Music

- "Glorify Thy Name"—**9:1**
  Words and music by Donna Adkins
  © 1976 Maranatha! Music

- "Great Is the Lord"—**4,9:1**
  Words and music by Michael W. Smith
  © 1982 Meadowgreen Music Co.

- "Hark the Herald Angels Sing"—**3**

- "Holy, Holy, Holy"—**4**

- "How Great Thou Art"—**4**

- "How Majestic Is Your Name"—**9:1**
  Words and music by Michael W. Smith
  © 1981 Meadowgreen Music

- "Humble Thyself"—**7:1**
  Words and music by Bob Hudson
  © 1978 Maranatha! Music

- "I Am the Resurrection and the Life"—**2,5:7**
  Words and music by Ray Repp
  © 1967 F.E.L. Publishers LTD.

- "I Believe in Jesus"—**1,2,5:2**
  Words and music by Marc Nelson
  © 1987 Mercy Publishing

- "I Stand in Awe"—**4:1**
  Words and music by Mark Altrogge
  © 1987 People of Destiny International/Pleasant Hills Music

- "I Walk by Faith"—**10:8**
  Words and music by Chris Falson
  © 1990 Seam of Gold. admin. by Maranatha! Music

- "It's Your Blood"—**1,7,8:2**
  Words and music by Michael Christ
  © 1985 Mercy Publishing

- "Jesus Mighty God"—**5:1**
  Words and music by Rick Founds
  © 1989 Maranatha! Music

- "Jesus Name above All Names"—**5:1**
  Words and music by Naida Hearn
  © 1974 Scripture in Song/Admin. by Maranatha! Music

- "Jesus, What a Wonder You Are"—**5:3**
  Words and music by Dave Bolton
  © 1975 Dawn Treader Music

- "Joy to the World"—3

- "Lion and the Lamb"—5:1
  Words and Music by Bill Batstone and Anne Barbour
  © 1990 Maranatha! Music

- "Lord, I Lift Your Name on High"—1,2,8:1
  Words and music by Rick Founds
  © 1989 Maranatha! Music

- "Majesty"—9:1
  Words and music by Jack Hayford
  © 1978 Lexicon

- "More Love, More Power"—6:4
  words and music by Jude Del Hirro
  © 1987 Mercy Publishing

- "More Precious than Silver"—3:1
  Words and music by Lynn DeShazzo
  © 1979 Integrity's Hosanna Music

- "My Peace"—11:3
  Words and music by Keith Routledge
  © 1975 and 1980, Kenwood Music

- "Nothing but the Blood of Jesus"—1,8
  Words and music by Robert Lowry

- "O Come, All Ye Faithful"—3

- "Oh, How He Loves You and Me"—1:1
  Kurt Kaiser
  © 1975 Word Music

- "O Little Town of Bethlehem"—3

- "Our God Is Faithful and Able"—10:1
  Words and music by Bob Fitts
  © 1991 Maranatha! Music

- "Peace Give I to Thee"—11:3
  Words and music by Vic Houser
  © 1972, Maranatha! Music

- "Search My Heart"—6,7,11:4
  words and music by Todd Collins and Rick Founds
  © 1982 Maranatha! Music

- "Shine, Jesus, Shine"—6:1
  words and music by Graham Kendrick
  © 1987 Make Way Music, Ltd.

- "Silent Night"—3

- "Spirit of God"—6:2
  words and music by Hanaeka Jacobs
  © 1984 Maranatha! Music

- "Spirit of the Living God (Fall afresh on me)"—6:1

- "Sweet Adoration"—9:11
  Words and music by Brown Bannister
  © 1980 Bug and Bear Music

- "The Steadfast Love of the Lord"—10:1
  Words and music by Edith McNeill
  © 1974 Celebration Services

- "There Is a Redeemer"—5:1
  Words and music by Keith Green
  © 1982 Birdwing Music/Cherry Lane Music Pub. Co. Admin. by Sparrow

- "What Child Is This?"—3

- "White as Snow"—1,7,8:1
  Words and music by Leon Olguin
  © 1990 Maranatha! Music

- "You Are My Hiding Place"—10:1
  Words and music by Michael Ledner
  © 1981 Maranatha! Music

- "You Are So Faithful"—10:1
  Maranatha! Praise Band
  © 1989 Maranatha! Music.

- "You Are the Vine"—5:2
  Words and music by Danny Daniels and Randy Rigby
  © 1985 Mercy Publishing

- "You Are the Mighty King"—4, 5:2
  words and music by Eddie Espinosa
  © 1982 Mercy Music

- "You Have Been Good"—10:6
  Words and music by Twila Paris
  © 1989 Ariose Music admin. by Word

- "You Have Broken the Chains"—2:5
  Words and Music by Jamie Owens-Collins
  © 1991 Fairhill Music, Inc.

Special Music

This list is of "special" music used in this book—that is, not group-singing songs, but performance pieces, solos, etc. The bold number that follows each song title indicates the worship service the song is used in.

"The Breath of Heaven (Mary's Song)"—**3**
by Chris Eaton and Amy Grant
Originally performed on Amy Grant's album *Home for Christmas*, Myrrh/A&M Records, 1992.

"Breathe on Me"—**6**
by Lowell Alexander and Billy Simon
© 1994 Birdwing Music and Sparrow Song
Recorded by Susan Ashton, Margaret Becker, and Christine Denté on the Sparrow album *Along the Road*; accompaniment track and music folio available.

"Down on My Knees"—**9**
Words and music by Wayne Kirkpatrick
© 1991 Emily Boothe, Inc. (BMI)
Administered by Reunion Music Group, Inc. As recorded by Susan Ashton on the Sparrow album, *Wakened by the Wind*; accompaniment track and music folio available.

"Fear Not, My Child" —**10**
Words and music by Carman
As recorded by Carman on the album *The Absolute Best*; accompaniment track by Word and music folio available.

"Glory to the Lamb"—**2**
Words and Music by Bill Batstone
© 1993 Maranatha! Music
As recorded on *Praise Band 4—Let the Walls Fall Down*; music book available.

"How Beautiful"—**7**
By Twila Paris
© 1990 Ariose Music
Originally recorded by Twila Paris on the album, *The Gift of Love*; accompaniment track available.

"How Can You Say No?"—**1**
Originally recorded by Julie Miller on the album "Meet Julie Miller"
Word, 1990. (Accompaniment available)
This song is also available as a music video on the video collection, *Command Performance* (Myrrh), as well as on *Edge TV—Edition 6* (Edge Communications, 800/616-EDGE).

"I Surrender All"—**8**
Words and music by David Moffitt and Regie Hamm
© 1992 Magnolia Hill Music
Originally recorded by Clay Crosse on *My Place Is with You* (Reunion Records); accompaniment track available.

"Messiah"—2
Words and music by John G. Elliot and Mark Baldwin
© 1986 Word Inc.
Recorded on the album *Undivided* by First Call. Music book and performance track available.

"The Peace That Passes Understanding "—11
Words and music by Wayne Watson and Claire Cloninger
© 1985 Word Music
Accompaniment track, music, and youth choral arrangements available.

"Sometimes He Calms the Storm"—11
Words and music by Scott Krippayne
© 1995 Word Music
Originally recorded by Scott Krippayne on the album *Wild Imagination*; accompaniment track available.

Videos

Here are the videos used in this book's worship services.

Service 1
- "Secret Ambition"
  From the album *I 2(Eye)* and featured on the video collection *Two x 4,* available from Reunion Records (1989). A popular youth video, it can be rented or ordered at most Christian bookstores.

- "How Can You Say No?"
  Suggested as special music in Service 1, but also available as a music video on the video collection, *Command Peformance* (Myrrh) as well as *Edge TV—Edition 6* (Youth Specialties/NavPress).

Service 5
- *Witness* by Curt Cloninger
  Available from Youth Specialties (800/776-8008).

- *Jesus* by Campus Crusade for Christ.
  Available at most Christian bookstores or can be ordered directly from Campus Crusade for Christ (800/827-2788).

Service 9
- *God Views* by Curt Cloninger
  Available from Youth Specialties (800/776-8008).

Youth Specialties Titles

Professional Resources

Developing Spiritual Growth in Junior High
   Students
Developing Student Leaders
Equipped to Serve: Volunteer Youth Worker
   Training Course
Help! I'm a Sunday School Teacher!
Help! I'm a Volunteer Youth Worker!
How to Expand Your Youth Ministry
How to Recruit and Train Volunteer Youth
   Workers
The Ministry of Nurture
One Kid at a Time
Peer Counseling in Youth Groups
Advanced Peer Counseling in Youth Groups

Discussion Starter Resources

Get 'Em Talking
4th-6th Grade TalkSheets
High School TalkSheets
Junior High TalkSheets
High School TalkSheets: Psalms and Proverbs
Junior High TalkSheets: Psalms and Proverbs
More High School TalkSheets
More Junior High TalkSheets
Parent Ministry TalkSheets
What If...? Provocative Questions to Get
   Teenagers Talking, Thinking, Doing
Would You Rather...? 465 Questions to Get Kids
   Talking

Ideas Library

Combos: 1-4, 5-8, 9-12, 13-16, 17-20, 21-24,
   25-28, 29-32, 33-36, 37-40, 41-44, 45-48,
   49-52
Singles: 53, 54, 55
Ideas Index

Youth Ministry Programming

Compassionate Kids: Practical Ways to Involve
   Kids in Mission and Service
Creative Bible Lessons in John: Encounters
   with Jesus
Creative Bible Lessons in Romans: Faith on
   Fire!
Creative Bible Lessons on the Life of Christ
Creative Programming Ideas for Junior High
   Ministry
Creative Socials and Special Events

Dramatic Pauses
Facing Your Future: Graduating Youth Group
   with a Faith That Lasts
Great Fundraising Ideas for Youth Groups
Great Retreats for Youth Groups
Greatest Skits on Earth
Greatest Skits on Earth, Vol. 2
Hot Illustrations for Youth Talks
More Hot Illustrations for Youth Talks
Hot Talks
Incredible Questionnaires for Youth Ministry
Junior High Game Nights
More Junior High Game Nights
Play It! Great Games for Groups
Play It Again! More Great Games for Groups
Road Trip
Super Sketches for Youth Ministry
Teaching the Bible Creatively
Up Close and Personal: How to Build
   Community in Your Youth Group

Clip Art

ArtSource Vol. 1—Fantastic Activities
ArtSource Vol. 2—Borders, Symbols, Holidays,
   and Attention Getters
ArtSource Vol. 3—Sports
ArtSource Vol. 4—Phrases and Verses
ArtSource Vol. 5—Amazing Oddities and
   Appalling Images
ArtSource Vol. 6—Spiritual Topics
ArtSource Vol. 7—Variety Pack
ArtSource CD-ROM (contains Vols. 1–7)

Videos

Edge TV
God Views
The Heart of Youth Ministry: A Morning
   with Mike Yaconelli
Next Time I Fall in Love Video Curriculum
Promo Spots for Junior High Game Nights
Understanding Your Teenager Video
   Curriculum

Student Books

Grow For It Journal
Grow For It Journal through the Scriptures
Wild Truth Journal for Junior Highers
101 Things to Do during a Dull Sermon